WISDOM
from the
WOODS

© Kenzie Cook of KC Photography, Superior, WI

About the Author

Mark Langenfeld earned his doctorate in clinical psychology from Alliant International University in Fresno, CA, in 2000. He's been teaching psychology and sociology at Northwood Technical College in Superior, WI, since 2006. Before teaching, he worked as a therapist for several years. Additionally, he presents workshops at conferences on various topics dealing with improving psychological well-being. His spiritual practices include Paganism and Buddhism. His hobbies include juggling, hiking, gardening, and meditation.

Praise for Wisdom from the Woods

"The author writes from not only his heart, but from his soul. Examples of events in his own life are paired with the lesson or lessons he learned, and examples of how the reader can include those practices in their own life. A book well worth adding to your library."

—**PAULA MORHARDT,** author of the Through the Garden Window series

"A power-packed supply of profound yet extremely commonsense wisdom. It's an all-purpose owner's manual on how to be human. Every page uses simple lessons from nature to show us how to be truer to ourselves, better with others, and how to live a life that's happier, healthier, and whole."

—**HELGA HEDGEWALKER,** artist and coauthor of *Color A Magick Spell*

"*Wisdom from the Woods* is written for all who seek to expand their sense of spiritual awareness by exploring their innate connection with Nature. With stories and images taken from everyday experiences, Dr. Langenfeld guides the reader in a friendly, conversational way."

—**PAUL B. RUCKER,** visionary artist

"Dr. Langenfeld is a professor of psychology whose writing is accessible enough to put anyone at ease. He uses simple language to discuss complex subjects and expresses deep wisdom in a very conversational style. *Wisdom from the Woods* is as delightful as it is thoughtful."

—**THRAICIE HAWKNER,** founder of The Eye of Horus shop

"A series of reflective observations of the experiences of nature that do not always unfold as expected. These reflective experiences bristle with implicit, occasionally explicit, suggestions of the paths to renewing oneself through one's connection with nature."

—**RICHARD DUUS, PhD,** author of *Thinking of Thinking*

"Long ago, humanity stopped listening to the rest of the world. In *Wisdom from the Woods*, Mark Langenfeld resumes the conversation."

—**STEVEN POSCH,** *The Paganistan Blog*

"Through a series of easy-to-read vignettes, *Wisdom from the Woods* uses real-life experiences to contextualize common problems and issues that face us all. Dr. Langenfeld's sincere interest in helping people achieve personal wellness is evident as he shares lessons learned through his appreciation for nature."

—**JOHN E. WILL, EdD**, President of Northwood Technical College

WISDOM from the WOODS

A YEAR OF GENTLE GUIDANCE FROM MOTHER NATURE

MARK LANGENFELD

WOODBURY, MINNESOTA

First Edition
First Printing, 2025

Book design by Rordan Brasington
Cover design by Kevin R. Brown
Interior illustrations by Llewellyn Art Department

Llewellyn Publications is a registered trademark of Llewellyn Worldwide Ltd.

Library of Congress Cataloging-in-Publication Data (Pending)
ISBN: 978-0-7387-8217-1

Llewellyn Publications
A Division of Llewellyn Worldwide Ltd.
2143 Wooddale Drive
Woodbury, MN 55125-2989
www.llewellyn.com

Printed in the United States of America

GPSR Representation:
UPI-2M PLUS d.o.o., Medulićeva 20, 10000 Zagreb, Croatia
matt.parsons@upi2mbooks.hr

Other Books by Mark Langenfeld

Hypnotic Pain Control for People Living with AIDS
(Doctoral dissertation published in 1999)

Forthcoming Books by Mark Langenfeld

Beyond Positive Thinking

Dedication

Everyone is both a student and a teacher. So, to all those students out there, I recognize and appreciate you. And to all those teachers who guided me over my lifetime, I honor you with a deep bow. Finally, I thank my two most influential teachers: Mother Nature, for providing wisdom through metaphors; and Buddha, for teaching me that I do not need to remember who I am—I need to forget who I thought I was.

Contents

Disclaimer

The opinions and statements in this book are for learning purposes only. When engaging in nature-based activities, caution should be taken to protect yourself and the environment by being mindful of your surroundings and refraining from touching wild animals, insects, and plants. Readers should always use their discretion.

The remarks given in this book should not be interpreted as psychological advice. This book is not a substitute for mental health therapy. Readers needing psychological assistance should seek a licensed therapist.

This book combines many general concepts, ideas, philosophies, and beliefs commonly shared worldwide. I am not claiming to have created any of these schools of thought. Thus, any similarities to preexisting philosophies are purely coincidental.

Introduction

The real-life stories in this book come from my firsthand experiences that demonstrate practical lessons and easy-to-understand wisdom learned from Mother Nature. This book takes a holistic view by combining self-development, psychological insight, and an understanding of your relationship with nature. Each chapter includes fresh suggestions to gently guide you toward personal wellness. Therefore, this book is designed to cultivate within you the motivation and encouragement needed to improve your life and discover the buried treasures within yourself.

The chapters of this book were intentionally designed to be read in any order that is best for you. You do not need to read them chronologically. The chapter titles give you a good description and preview of the upcoming content. Thus, you are invited to choose the topics you desire anytime. There are fifty-two chapters, so you can read one chapter each week for a year as an inspirational study if that suits your needs.

The lessons in this book are highly adaptable to any situation or life circumstance. Nature's wisdom applies to you regardless of your beliefs, culture, education, age, sex, or lifestyle. Everyone can relate to nature because we are all living on this planet. What lessons will you learn from this book?

1

Who Pooped on My Path to Enlightenment?

Sometimes, we think the universe has it in for us. Nothing is going our way. And when we think things can't get any worse, they do! That's when we want to crawl into bed, cover our heads with a blanket, and hope for a better tomorrow.

But now is not the time to run and hide; it is the time to lean into the challenge and learn from it. When things seem wrong, we must remind ourselves that no one is perfect. What appears to be a mistake at first could be an excellent opportunity for improvement down the road.

Case in point: I have a special area in the woods where I like to sit and meditate. It's a beautiful place right under a huge pine tree. A small creek flows by just a few yards away. I sit under the sheltering boughs of this mighty tree and listen to the peaceful sounds of the water trickling past. It's a tranquil spot where I can clear my mind of all my cares.

One summer day, I went to my special place only to discover that, much to my chagrin, an animal had defecated precisely where I usually sit. Ugh! I was mad. I figured out that the speckled excrement must have been from a black bear because it was full of raspberry seeds, a favorite treat for black bears.

This was particularly ironic and personally insulting because the black bear is spiritually significant to me. (How crazy is that, right!?) So, what does it mean when an animal I admire leaves a hot, steaming pile of compost in my private paradise? That's a question for the sages.

I could think of no answer, at least not at first. Life seemed to pull a little prank on me to see if I was paying attention or getting complacent. In any case, at the time, it didn't make sense to me.

I reflected on this new mystery that destiny so quaintly put in my path. From the stillness of my mind, the thought came to me that perhaps this foul-smelling disturbance was a gentle reminder (albeit humorous) that everything changes; nothing stays the same. So, I chose another beautiful place to sit peacefully until the revolting heap of ick decayed.

Months later, I returned to see if the cleansing rain had purified the defilement from my prior sanctuary spot. Surprisingly, the compost had become black dirt, and new green raspberry sprouts grew there. What started as something disgusting (at least according to my human values) was now something beautiful. New life came from the dead matter. That was the answer I sought when I asked the universe what all this had meant.

I understand now that nature has a purpose for everything. It may not be apparent initially, but it will reveal itself eventually. The trick is to be patient. And that is what I intend to do; I will be patient and wait for those raspberry sprouts to grow into full bushes that bear (no pun intended) fruit. Perhaps in a couple of years, I'll be able to sit in my tranquil space by the creek and pick some plump, juicy raspberries to enjoy on my path to enlightenment.

Today's Teaching from Mother Nature

If you don't have a quiet place to sit, please find one. It doesn't have to be a place in the woods. Your desk, cubicle, garage, bedroom, or private area can suffice. In a jam, even a five-minute bathroom break will do if a lock on the door prevents anyone from barging in on you.

Once you find a peaceful place, close your eyes, take a deep breath, and enter a tranquil mental state. Breathe in tranquility; breathe out understanding. Quiet your mind and embrace the stillness. Contemplate some personal questions and reflect on their meaning.

Give some thought to those moments when you believed everything was going wrong. How did things improve? Or if they haven't yet, how could they? What if you looked at the situation in a different light? If you viewed the so-called problem from the long-term perspective of Mother Nature, how would things look then?

What if you adjusted your thoughts and started thinking of the problem as an opportunity in disguise? How might that feel? Would you feel more energized to work on turning that problem into an opportunity? Would your new, positive attitude give you the fresh perspective you seek? In other words, can you find fresh green sprouts popping up from the compost in your life?

2

My Dog Is More Forgiving than I Am

Before my dog passed, I used to watch her on the lawn. She would lie on her back, enjoying the warm sun on her belly. Even though she was in the final stage of her life and had arthritis, partial blindness, and deafness, she still seemed to enjoy life. Lying on the grass, she was entirely in the moment and living life to the fullest. I realized that I have a lot to learn from my dog.

I recall other times when my dog taught me life lessons, such as when she got into barking fights with other dogs. During those conflicts, the fur on her shoulders and rump stood up. This made her look fiercer than she was. She growled and showed her teeth like a dominant alpha wolf. No blood was shed; it was all just defensive posturing. My dog never bit anything other than dog food.

What caught my interest was the quickness in which she shook it off—literally! When the growling match was over, and the two dogs went their separate ways, she shook her fur from head to tail. It looked like she was releasing all the residual tension from that canine confrontation in one good body shake. And then, she was fine again, wagging her tail and trotting along merrily as if the whole incident was behind her—which it was.

That was the lesson—when the danger passes, leave anger behind by living in the present. Let it go; the past has passed. It's a message most of us have heard before. Do we practice it?

The other day, a customer service clerk treated me less than respectfully. Since I cannot read minds, I honestly do not know if she meant her comments to be disrespectful to me. However, I felt offended and ruminated about the incident for the rest of the day. I could not figure out why she was so rude. After all, it's part of her job to be courteous. As I mentally replayed the incident, I felt my face getting hot.

But, hey, is that what my dog did? No! She shook it off as soon as the offender was out of sight. She forgot the whole incident within seconds, not days. That's the benefit of being fully in the present moment. I must learn how to do that. The way I respond to something is my choice. I always have the option to shrug it off.

That's not the only lesson my dog taught me. I also noticed that she was quick to forgive and did not harbor feelings of resentment. In the past, when I needed to scold her, she looked guilty; her tail tucked between her legs, and her ears drooped. However, as soon as I changed my tone to a more affectionate baby talk, she immediately came running to me with her tail wagging and prancing her paws on the ground in what looked like a doggie dance.

I need to learn that type of quick forgiveness for my life. How many times have I held on to my hurt feelings because I allowed myself to be offended that someone corrected a mistake I'd made, and I'd felt embarrassed? Or how about the countless times I felt resentful because a friend or romantic partner pointed out some flaw in my behavior? It's far better for everyone to forgive minor transgressions as quickly as my easygoing pet.

Let me be clear: Forgiveness does not imply that what the offender did was okay, especially in severe cases. Forgiveness is for freeing yourself from resentment. It does not mean the offender is freed from accountability.

Today's Teaching from Mother Nature

Picture a lovable doggie when you get frustrated, angry, or upset. Recall how a friendly pooch can shake off a negative experience. And then, immediately afterward, the dog goes about life without ruminating on the confrontation that just ended.

Allow yourself to forgive minor offenses as quickly as a dog does. Let bygones be bygones. Once you have let go of past hurts, you can greet the people you love with the warm reception a dog gives when you come home. And if you are bold enough, take a moment to roll around on your back on the lawn and let the sun warm your belly. Who cares what the neighbors think? They're probably envious of your uninhibited personality.

3
Insight Gained from Mother Nature

As we explore the wisdom of nature, it is beneficial to first release preconceived notions and be open-minded to new ideas. Most of us, including myself, fall into a kind of mental trap. In other words, once we embrace an opinion about something, we only look for information that confirms our opinion.

That said, it stands to reason that if we want to open our minds, we need to free ourselves from what we already think we know. Learning to unlearn our dogmatic beliefs is a mental acknowledgment that we all have much to understand about any topic.

I first discovered this lesson when I was finishing my doctoral program. It was a humbling experience to realize that even though I had the degree to show expertise in my field, I still had much more to learn. I could never know it all, regardless of my credentials. I soon realized that people will not care how much I know until they know how much I care. I keep that in mind as I counsel and teach people.

I thought about the intelligence of Mother Earth and how She does not try to be wise. That is what makes Her truly wise. There is a difference between possessing knowledge and having wisdom. The latter encompasses compassion. Without compassion, raw knowledge could be misused to exploit others.

We can learn to trust the earth and let Mother Nature run Her course without human interference. It seems that things worsen when humans try to control nature's forces. Learning to adapt and adjust to natural forces would be far better. When we embrace the planet as it is without trying to change it, the wisdom of the earth will be in our hearts. Perhaps then, we will better understand our human nature.

Why do some people want to change nature? Could they be projecting their flaws? If people believe they need improvement, they may project that issue onto nature in a futile attempt to supposedly *correct* the earth. However, this endeavor is an impossible mission because humans cannot improve the wisdom of nature. If people meddle with the natural order of things, they could damage it. And if people try to exploit the earth for selfish gains, they could disrupt the delicate balance of nature. Intelligent people learn from nature and grow wiser. Irrational people try to control nature and fail.

Whenever people disturb the laws of nature, devastation eventually ensues. This has been seen countless times throughout human history. The smog and carbon polluting the air, toxic waste dumped into the soil, litter scattered across the land, oil spills contaminating water supplies, and devastation of wildlife are all consequences of human interference with the natural order.

As a positive step, we all need to follow the wisdom of nature to save ourselves; this requires us to practice humility, which is not a very popular subject among humans. None of us are superior to nature. We are part of nature, not above it. We are all organic and, therefore, subject to the same laws of nature as every other being on the planet. Our bodies will grow old, die, and decay, just like the decomposing leaves on our lawns. How's that for a sobering image to keep us humble?

If we let go of our self-defeating beliefs, nature can guide us. One of the many things the earth can teach us is how to be yielding. When the wind blows, what happens? The trees sway, the tall grass bends, and the clouds peacefully drift across the sky. We, too, can learn to roll with the punches. As we face the trials and tribulations of the day, let's be flexible and yield to the laws of nature. Resisting the natural order is analogous to a child resisting physical growth.

Everything has its time. The morning light eventually turns into evening light, only to repeatedly perform the same cycle the next day. Life is a circle, and we will someday return our bodies to the earth. The sun is not in a hurry; it does not need to rush. We need to take that lesson from Mother Nature and slow down.

Today's Teaching from Mother Nature

The more we resist nature, the more we produce stress. So, cooperate with the natural order of things. Pay attention to the cycles of nature. Notice the current season. Is the earth sleeping in winter, just awakening in spring, or growing and flourishing in summer? Or is the earth preparing to slow down and yield its harvest as it does in the fall? What is nature trying to teach you in this current season? Having open-mindedness and a greater awareness of nature is the first step in understanding the wisdom of the earth.

4
The Kindhearted Grandmother Moon

The conflicts of life can sometimes be overwhelming. With so many people displaying anger around us and all the problems we hear about daily, it is no wonder we occasionally retreat into the protective fortress of our inner selves. (I empathize.) That's the way life goes sometimes. We cannot expect every person we meet to be warm and friendly. Sooner or later, we will meet someone in a bad mood who vents anger at us. The big question is what to do about it. How do we respond? Often, our fear and anxiety wage war in our heads.

Here is a visualization exercise that can sketch your negative thoughts and feelings into a mental portrait: Imagine a castle with a protective fortress in front of it. Notice what a dark and dreary picture your pessimistic thinking has painted in your mind's eye. This portrait is an example of what cynicism can do to you.

Picture walking out into the courtyard and seeing the dismal-looking day. The sky is gray and overcast, with black clouds churning overhead. There is a noticeable absence of color. Everything seems black and white with different shades of gray. Glancing around the enclosure, you see the combat damage on the massive stone walls that enclose this conceptual castle. Deep fractures cover the exterior of your fortress from the emotional battles it withstood.

As the evening light casts long, lonely shadows across your castle, you feel empty and alone. That's when you realize it is essential to get out of your head occasionally and talk with other caring human beings who can help give you some perspective. Otherwise, this castle can become a barrier from which no one can reach you. You understand that if you emotionally withdraw and isolate too much, the drawbridge on your castle could grow immobile from lack of use, and the hinges might rust shut.

As we continue with this visualization, please observe that the pale and ragged battle flag still flaps in the wind but does not symbolize triumph. Wandering through the courtyard, you walk cautiously for fear of falling prey to the snares you set out to trap the people with whom you fight and argue. You see the tarnished bodies of the tin warriors that litter the grounds. They are remnants of the clashes you had with your so-called adversaries you created in your mind. This psychological fortress protects you from the people who might hurt you with their sharp words, piercing ridicule, and cutting rejection. Unfortunately, a part of you gets misplaced in the process.

We all have defense mechanisms. As children, we begin to build these structures and continue to reinforce them over the years. Typically, we hide from emotional threats by mentally going inside ourselves. Then, we cover up how we feel by pretending to be someone we are not. Actions such as this are ultimately counterproductive because they cause us to go deeper into the castle of our inner selves. If taken to the extreme, we can become lost in the maze of our minds. Sadly, the price we pay for building the mental fortress is all too often that we become a prisoner of our defenses.

At this point, you may be wondering what we can do to improve this situation. (I'm glad you asked.) To escape from this self-made mental structure, we need to make the firm decision to leave. Then, make a great effort to reach the outside and begin the journey of emotional liberation. We can turn the tide. This mental war must be waged against the fortress, not against the people. We can start tearing down the castle brick by brick and build a new bridge that connects us to others.

Try this fresh, positive visualization that paints a much more pleasing picture: Instead of viewing life as a battle, find tranquility in the calming beauty of nature. To seek temporary solace from the challenges of everyday life, close your eyes and picture yourself standing in a grassy field on a warm summer night. Look up at the full moon. Imagine that the moon looks like the face of a kindhearted grandmother. She is a gentle and understanding soul who comforts you. You feel happy and safe in this place. Her smiling face shines beams of whitish-blue moonlight down onto you. Bask in this hazy aura.

Imagine hearing Grandmother Moon calling your name. Answer that call before the image fades in the morning light. She hangs in the night sky waiting for you. Looking across the windblown fields, you see the moonbeams dancing like fairies on the petals of the night flowers. Slowly, Grandmother Moon travels across the dark sky, watching over you while you sleep. She is your protector. What emotion are you experiencing right now as you envision this scene?

Imagine seeing yourself as a very young child crawling up to Grandmother Moon and extending your arms, wanting to be picked up. She has been with you your whole life, so the two of you have a familiarity and comfort level. Her lap cradles you with soft, pale moonlight that gently wraps around you like a huggable blanket. She is patient and never grows tired of you. How do you feel at this moment? I bet life doesn't seem as harsh now.

Today's Teaching from Mother Nature

Designate at least thirty minutes each day for silence and stillness. Call a ceasefire in the battle of life. Come out of that mental castle where you seek refuge when you feel threatened by the anger of other people.

Each night this week, utilize this visualization exercise of Grandmother Moon and see if you feel more relaxed and sleep more peacefully. As a bonus, you might even have some interesting dreams. If you do, journal on it.

5
People Are Interconnected Like Trees

I am mindful of how bare the woods look during the winter season. The leaves have fallen off the trees, and the brilliant colors of fall seem to fade to dull shades of brown, gray, tan, and white. At first glance, when I look at a grove of trees, they appear to be standing independently from each other with their trunks spaced apart. However, when I look up higher, I notice that the branches interconnect and touch. The trees are separate yet joined. They are individuals yet a community.

It is the same way with people. We may be individuals enriched by our respective cultures, yet we branch out and touch each other's lives in multiple ways. From the products we buy to the environmental concerns, we all affect one another to some degree.

During my first year in graduate school, I volunteered to counsel students with emotional and behavioral problems at a local middle school. Many of those young people were members of rival gangs who often got into fights at school. When I was counseling a group of those students, we usually left the classroom and walked around the campus grounds. I asked them to observe how the trees in the courtyard were all spaced evenly apart and how the branches were interwoven toward the top. The trees were all different, yet they lived together side by side. I utilized this courtyard scene as a metaphor to exemplify multicultural connectedness. If the trees can live together despite their differences, so can we.

Being connected involves being part of a community. And being part of a community includes helping each other. We all need to lean on one another occasionally. A visible depiction of this social lesson came to me while hiking in the Sierra Mountains when I saw a boulder leaning on a giant conifer's trunk. This unlikely pairing of stone and pine tree caught my eye, and I stopped to take a minute to contemplate its meaning.

Softly, a thought settled on my mind as gently as the freshly fallen mountain snow. I realized there may be times when I need to lean on others, and others may need to lean on me. Countless hikers undoubtedly passed by this same scene. I couldn't help but wonder how many of them noticed the rock and tree duo and considered it a metaphor for how we all need to support one another.

It's amazing how Mother Nature speaks to us when we understand Her language. For example, while walking through the woods one evening, I heard the wind blowing strongly through the trees. The limbs from two trees rubbed against one another, making a high-pitched squeak. Then, on the other side of me, I heard a different tree making a much lower creaking sound. Back and forth they went. In my imagination, it seemed like they were talking to each other. They each seemed to have their unique voice. I learned from this experience that people are not the only creatures with language; trees also have their way of communicating—if you tune in to their frequency.

One way that trees protect each other is when the older trees provide shade to shield the vulnerable younger saplings from the scorching sun. If you transplant one of these saplings from the shade to an open field, it will soon wither and die. The mature trees help the saplings slowly get accustomed to the indirect sunlight until the young ones are tall and strong enough to handle the direct sunlight. By the time the older trees are ready to die and fall, the younger trees are prepared to stand on their own. The lesson here is clear—children need mentors.

Speaking of protection, have you seen the damage that porcupines can do to a tree? They will eat up the tender new growth on a tree. They don't seem interested in the thicker bark around the trunk, only the younger, more vulnerable, bark. Just one porcupine can cause severe damage or even destroy a tree overnight. Do you know a porcupine-type person who tried to ruin your vulnerable personal growth with criticism? It's as though that prickly person was eating your progress. Do you know anyone at work like that? Your inner tree needs protection from growth-robbing porcupines.

So, how can you protect your inner tree from predation? Some tree nurseries use unique tree wraps to protect the trunks of young trees from harm. Similarly, you can create a mental barrier by wrapping yourself in wisdom so that your inner tree is guarded with factual knowledge, not false rumors.

Today's Teaching from Mother Nature

Be as socially connected as the trees in the forest. The branches are interconnected even though the trees stand apart. Similarly, you can still be an individual while simultaneously being linked to our multicultural community.

6
Empathic Breathing Intercession

The news is full of heartache and human misery. Stories are reported almost daily about war, starvation, disease, floods, hurricanes, and more. You can hardly read a headline or watch the television without having tales of tragedies thrown in your face. It is easy to feel overwhelmed and helpless. But do not become complacent and jaded. When you hear of the pain of others, you may find yourself wondering what you can do to help them. Although you may not be able to go to them to render aid physically, there is an act of empathy you can do to send them positive energy.

I use a breathing technique, which I refer to as empathic intervention. Here's what you do: Try breathing in love from the universe and breathing out compassion for those who suffer. You may wonder what good this will do. Well, for one thing, it teaches you to be a more compassionate person. Every time you breathe compassion for another person, you expand your capacity for empathy. It also gives you more emotional stability because you do not feel so helpless when you hear about human misery. The positive energy you breathe out to people could emotionally benefit them on a metaphysical level. Perhaps their distress will slightly decrease when they receive enough positive energy—in whatever form.

If you like, you can view this empathic breathing exercise as a form of prayer. It does not matter what you call it. Focus on loving other people actively. Talking about love is not the same as doing something loving. Breathing may seem passive, but it is not. Breathing is action, and breathing empathy for those in need is one way to practice love.

Say, for instance, you hear on the national news that a young person in another state died in a car accident. Now, their surviving family and friends are in tremendous emotional pain. Instead of turning away and doing something to take your mind off the sad news, you can take that opportunity to breathe compassion out to those who are in mourning by practicing psychic intervention.

Furthermore, what if a coworker dumps all her emotional baggage on you? You know you cannot solve the problems for her. However, you can be empathetic and listen to her concerns. As you do, breathe in her pain. Let your love for humanity convert that pain into positive energy in your heart. Then, as you are still listening to her, breathe out compassion.

Maybe it is an international situation where people are starving or experiencing some horrible disease. If a relief fund is set up, you could donate some money to help them. Additionally, you can breathe emotional relief to them with your loving thoughts. Being compassionate only takes a minute of your time.

This exercise in sympathy can also work to reduce and control the frustration you feel toward others. Imagine that your child comes home from school with an unsatisfactory grade. Your desire for them to get a much higher grade could easily lead to frustration.

Moreover, acting on this frustration could lead to confrontation. You might yell something about how your child should know better or that you expect more. You might accidentally say something hurtful, like, "What is wrong with you?" And then, you may top it off with a condemning comment about how you didn't raise your child to be like this. These injurious words will not strengthen the bond you have with your youngster. It will only drive a wedge between the two of you.

What if you took a few moments to gather your thoughts before speaking instead of displaying frustration? (Okay, let's call that a *timeout*. We can work with that overused catchword, can't we?) Using the empathic breathing technique, you can put yourself in the other person's shoes and better understand the situation. It is possible that despite your kid's best efforts, the grade still fell short of parental expectations. A more likely explanation might be that the schoolwork or the exam was not a proper vehicle by which to measure your child's knowledge accurately. This is usually the case.

Understanding leads to compassion. Once you know more about the reason for the low grade, you can bring yourself to an emotional state of peace. You can take that slow, deep breath and exhale compassion to your youngster. That type of empathy leads to a stronger parent-child relationship.

Today's Teaching from Mother Nature

When you are home tonight watching the news, be sensitive to the suffering of others. As you learn about their struggles, imagine being in their situation. Feel for them. As you do this, breathe in love from the universe and exhale compassion to those who suffer. The more you do this mystical breathing to practice empathic intervention, the more compassionate you become. And the world sure needs more compassionate people right now.

7

Raindrops Have the Present Moment

Raindrops last only briefly as they fall to the earth and are absorbed by the thirsty soil. Similarly, your lifetime is limited, too. When your time is up, your life energy is absorbed back into the universe like a raindrop. You are not guaranteed the future; you only have the present moment. Therefore, when you work, it helps to be mindful that whatever you do is only temporarily valuable because nothing lasts forever. So, enjoy every moment.

My guess is you work hard, don't you? I'm curious, though… what thoughts go through your mind when you are working so diligently? For me, two thoughts guide my sense of work ethic. First, I pretend that whatever I am doing is the most valuable task in the whole world. Second, I realize that whatever I am doing will not last an eternity.

Does that sound like contradictory thoughts? Well, maybe at first. However, what if we dig a little deeper to discover what lies beneath the surface of those two thoughts? The confusion comes from our perspective of time. It's not an issue of *what* matters; it's an issue of *when* it matters.

Perhaps an example would help. A while back, I was doing some yard work. I looked over my property and noticed all the chores, repairs, half-finished projects, and piles of various materials. These outdoor projects had accumulated over the years, and it was about time things got done. I worked on them for many hours. It was hard labor, which involved shoveling piles of dirt, moving lumber, and lifting large stones and other heavy materials. I continued to work until the dim twilight sky made it too dark to see what I was doing.

While washing up at the kitchen sink, I wondered why I had worked so extra hard. After drying my hands on my favorite pastel green dish towel, I thought about those two work-related thoughts described earlier. The two are not conflicting thoughts if viewed from a timeline perspective. Most personal accomplishments feel important at the time they are achieved. However, those same accomplishments will not matter in the eternal timeline. The work I did that day only mattered in the short term. It will not matter a thousand years from now—neither will I.

That is why it is so crucial to live and work in the present moment; that's all we have. Everything we build will eventually be torn down. Whatever we design, paint, write, or make will ultimately come to an end. I'm not trying to dampen your mood here; I do, however, want to emphasize the importance of appreciating the gift of now. Don't let time slip away. What matters right now is working together and building deep friendships.

All living organisms eventually die, decompose, and transform into something else, like soil, air, gas, water, ashes, and so on. That is how things are, the way they are meant to be. Call it the law of nature, if you will. The human body was not physically designed to regenerate cells indefinitely. Some say death is sad and depressing. But really, that is just the egotistical voice of human arrogance, which thinks people should live forever. It's just a fact that everything ultimately decomposes and becomes other things. It is neither good nor bad; it just is. If you try to deny or fear the inevitable natural conclusion of life, you produce unnecessary stress and anxiety. Is that how you want to spend your time?

Today's Teaching from Mother Nature

Raindrops are here and gone. Nothing lasts forever. Yet, they are valuable in the present moment. Likewise, you are important and matter in the here and now. Once you appreciate yourself, you can also value other people in your current life. Give the people you care about a hug. Do it today! Don't wait until tomorrow.

You have no assurance that you will be able to show your appreciation in the future because the future never arrives; it is always the current moment. When that long-awaited future date comes, it is not the future anymore; now, it is the present. You have no guaranteed future. And like the raindrops falling to earth, time is fleeting. Act as though whatever you're doing now is the most valuable thing in the world, at least temporarily.

8

No Shame in a Songbird's Game

Are you as perfectly flawed as I am? There comes a time when we must embrace the realization that our flaws are only viewed as defects if we are trying to live up to the expectations of others. Our society constantly bombards us with messages telling us how they want us to be, ranging from the clothes we wear to our body type. Society conveys to us that we are unacceptable the way we are naturally. The not-so-subtle message is that they want us to change, or they will withhold social approval.

Unfortunately, that approval comes at a high cost. We feel like frauds when we abandon our true nature and try to be someone else. This news should come as no surprise. After all, we sometimes fake our true feelings in social situations. So, of course, we will feel phony under those circumstances. After a while, the lonely feeling of losing touch with the person we were born to be grows within us. That's when we start to wonder if the high cost of social approval is worth it.

On the flip side, what about the cost of social rejection? To be true to your nature may mean not fitting in. It also may mean being left out, overlooked, ignored, verbally attacked, or even subjected to physical violence. We need only look back at history to find ample examples of cruelty from groups in power that inflicted suffering on those who did not conform.

It is at times like this when I like to think about songbirds. Although they share similar traits, each bird is unique. Despite their diversity, they do not feel inferior to one another. Each boldly sings a song without looking to the left or right for approval. I have enjoyed listening to songbirds for years and have yet to see even one of them blush with embarrassment over singing a note off-key. They don't worry about it. They unapologetically belt out their tunes for the world to hear. (Critics be damned!)

It sounds a bit kitschy or cliché to talk about a person's inner light, but that is what I imagine when I think about an individual's inner beauty. I have always been a visual thinker. Maybe it's because of my dyslexia. Even as a small child, I can remember looking at all the different colored houses in the bright sunlight and noticing how beautiful each one was outside. Then, when my family drove past those identical houses after dark, I noticed the homes looked a little different; I could no longer see the outside as well. What caught my attention was that some of the houses were glowing and lit up from the inside. Other homes were dark.

Now, when I drive past houses at night, I think about how people, like houses, may look pretty on the outside. However, if they don't let their inner light glow, they cannot be distinguished from the darkness; they are invisible. I don't know about you, but I don't want to be invisible.

On a personal note, let me share the lessons I've learned in prison. No, I was not locked up; I was teaching a psychology class in a prison for a semester. Here is what stood out: The staff who trained me during my weeklong orientation said I should act stern and strict when dealing with the criminal offenders and prisoners in my class. I was told not even to smile because it might show weakness. In other words, the trainers asked me to be someone I am not.

My entire life, I resisted the pressure to change my true nature or to conform to the expectations of others. In my psychology profession, I encourage people to be authentic. Yet ironically, the authority figures at the prison expected me to be inauthentic while teaching a psychology class that promotes authenticity. Well, I am not that good of an actor; the only role I can play is myself. Besides, many of the incarcerated men who took my class were most likely quite astute at reading people and picking up a fake façade.

After some quiet contemplation, I decided to be myself and keep things real. As it turned out, being genuine was the best choice. I believe the class received me well because I showed them basic human dignity and I was authentic. I did not attempt to hide my flaws, and I admitted that I, like them, was not perfect. How refreshing it must have been for them to be with someone who looked them in the eye and gave a sincere smile. They treated me with the same respect I showed them.

Today's Teaching from Mother Nature

You have an inner light. Like the songbirds, you, too, have unique gifts, talents, and abilities. Do you honestly think you were born to live someone else's life? You are on a unique path in life. Please don't fall into the trap the media lays out for you when they make it seem like you are not pretty, thin, or strong enough. I suggest you try thinking of your imperfections as gifts that build character. See how that new outlook improves the way you feel.

9

At Peace with the Storm in Your Head

Oh, the plight of the troubled mind. It's like a thunderstorm in the brain. Typically, when you are feeling disturbed, it's not the actual situation that bothers you—it's the negative emotions you attach to that event. Let me say that again. The pessimistic appraisal you attach to an incident produces negative feelings. The underlying problem is that you do not feel at peace within yourself. If you did, you would not feel the need to change the outside world to fit your inner world.

Picturesque as your inner world may seem, it is imperative to accept the natural order of life and let go of trying to be the master of the universe. When your life is out of harmony with the natural world, you become out of whack and start flailing as you grasp for something outside yourself to bring a sense of balance back into your life. When you are out of touch with nature, you are out of flow. It's analogous to your canoe getting stuck on a sandbar when trying to float down the river. That's what it is like to be out of flow.

Yet, it appears the human mind is constantly trying to solve problems. Think about it. As soon as you got up this morning, you probably started focusing on problem-solving thoughts. How much time do you have before leaving the house? What will you have for breakfast? What do you want to wear? What do you need to do today?

And isn't it true that when your mind solves one problem, it finds another? You look around and wonder if you can find something that is not right or needs changing. When was the last time you had no problems for your mind to solve? Is your mind ever content? When is your mind ever at rest?

Here's a fresh idea: Just for a moment, give your mind a well-deserved sabbatical and let things be. Try not to solve anything just for a few minutes. Can you do that? Don't try too hard now, or you will turn this little, not-solving-anything task into a problem to solve.

Please understand that I am not saying you should ignore your problems by living in denial. On the contrary, it is far better emotionally if you recognize that some things are within your control, such as your behavior, and some are out of your control, such as Mother Nature. So, stop struggling with natural events beyond your power. When birds see the gathering dark rain clouds, they don't try to stop the storm; they seek shelter.

Ultimately, you can only control your attitude and behavior. World events are entirely out of your hands. Therefore, accept the inevitable and face reality. Sometimes, realities can be challenging, such as aging, hazardous weather, world catastrophes, or rush hour, which is my pet peeve.

Side note—I must admit, it has been a fantasy of mine to control that one slow driver at the head of the traffic jam. You know what I'm talking about; it's the one who causes everyone else to be late. Sometimes, if I squint, I can see that slowpoke ahead with the brake lights on. If I were in control of the universe, I'd order a spaceship to hover over the slow vehicle to beam the driver up. Wouldn't that be nice? (Sigh.)

You see, we play this kind of mind game all the time. We have preconceived notions about how we think the world should be. We try to solve our inner problems with external things. However, external fixes for internal issues don't work. Come on; we can't expect our minds to fix everything. So why do we torture ourselves by engaging in that mental struggle? Why not just acknowledge that some things are out of our hands and let them go? A sense of peace comes from accepting the way Mother Nature intended things. Find calm in the eye of the storm. At first read, that pithy little phrase may seem to be common sense. However, how many of us put it into practice?

All too often, what ends up happening is that you cognitively reconstruct the outside world inside your mind in a way that fits your preconceived notions. You subconsciously do this because you desire a feeling of control, and you are, after all, the prime ruler of the world in your head. And once that cognitive task is neatly done, all that's left for you to do is live in your sublime mental world. Come to think of it, emotionally, you have nowhere else to live except in your mental world.

It's like this: Your inner thoughts are a running dialog of your moment-by-moment experiences. For example, you are walking across a dimly lit parking lot one night, and your inner voice tells you it is very dark out here. But you already know it is dark, so why does your inner voice keep repeating that message? It's your mind's way of giving you a false sense of control over the outside world. It's like waiting for an elevator, and you repeatedly push the button on the wall as if that will help. You keep doing it to feign control.

Today's Teaching from Mother Nature

The next time you catch yourself trying to solve your inner problems with outside solutions, notice how you are not solving the problem of lacking inner peace. Instead, what you are attempting to do is avoid unpleasant emotions such as anxiety. To address your internal issues, go beyond your comfort zone and lean into your emotions. Face your feelings as an alternative to avoiding them. Then, take a deep breath and finally let your problem-solving mind be at peace. Exhale.

10

Behavioral Pruning Yields Fruit

Recently, I was pruning my apple trees. I noticed how my alterations on the trees mirrored the behavioral modifications people sometimes make when working on personal issues. This analogy applies whether in a counseling session or when working on self-improvement independently.

To understand this metaphor, it is necessary first to understand the pruning procedure. Ideally, pruning should be done when the branch is very young. To prune a young branch is to train it. The goal, of course, is to improve the apple tree's production. Proper pruning also makes for a more vigorous tree because branches that are developing in an unhealthy way can be very destructive to the entire tree if allowed to continue.

Take, for example, two branches that cross each other close enough that they touch. When the wind blows, and the branches sway back and forth, they rub against each other, causing bark damage and scars. When the protective bark is torn open, the tree's defense system is compromised, leaving it susceptible to fungal problems and insect infestation.

Likewise, when you are working on changing some of your destructive habits, it is ideal to prune these maladaptive behaviors while they are still new. Young behaviors are relatively easy to change. Like the branches of a tree, you are training your behavior not to cross other people or rub someone the wrong way. Whether pruning a tree or a bad habit, the goal remains to increase strength and productivity.

Conversely, it is tough to prune a problematic branch after waiting several years because it has become a limb and is well established. That malformed limb is now large and heavy; pruning it is a significant undertaking. And if you try to prune more than one large limb per year, you risk having the entire tree go into shock. When this happens, the tree may not produce any fruit that year.

People with older, well-established behavioral patterns find it just as challenging to prune away those nasty habits. Working as a counselor, I taught people behavior modification techniques. I discovered that, like the large limbs of a tree, if a client tried to remove more than one deeply established behavioral pattern at a time, the client became emotionally overwhelmed and less productive. That is why it is best to spread the biggest behavioral pruning over a long period, even years.

Why don't we take a realistic look at how this type of behavioral pruning can play a practical role in someone's life? What if an average person (let's call him Bill) has a bad habit of interrupting others? If Bill had aimed to prune away this nonproductive behavior, his first step would have been identifying when he typically interrupts people. Although there may be several places where this behavior manifests itself, we will concentrate on the work environment.

The next step is for Bill to become more aware of when he does this behavior. Raising awareness of the problem is crucial for getting a handle on it. Perhaps Bill has noticed that while at staff meetings, he has difficulty waiting until people finish their statements before he speaks his mind. Once Bill detects this maladaptive behavior, he will see it more frequently, probably much more than he wants to admit.

The final step is the big one—the pruning! The next time Bill feels the urge to interrupt, he can train himself to jot down his thoughts on paper instead of impulsively blurting them out. Although it may take time, eventually, he will condition himself to wait for an appropriate moment to speak. This new habituation does not happen overnight, so Bill must also be patient with himself. Eventually, he will discover that, just like training an apple tree, he can prune off some of his dysfunctional habits individually.

Today's Teaching from Mother Nature

Think about a time when you had difficulty interacting with another person. Review this problem in your mind and see if you can identify the specific behavior that contributed to the problem. Perhaps it was your criticism, hostility, impatience, indifference, pessimism, accusing attitude, or something else.

Do not get distracted by looking for fault with the other person involved in this conflict. This exercise focuses on improving your behavior, not pointing your finger at anyone. Remember, you can only change yourself. You cannot force anyone else to change.

The next step is to pick one of the behaviors you believe is dysfunctional; this is that bad habit you most want to prune. Take a piece of paper and write down this behavior modification. Make it a personal goal. Then, work on that objective until you have succeeded. Remove the old behavior as if you were pruning a nonproductive branch that doesn't produce fruit.

At this point, a visualization exercise might assist you in this personal improvement process. In your mind, see yourself as a beautiful tree, strong and sturdy. Imagine this bad habit of yours as a dead branch you need to eliminate because it serves no functional purpose. Picture this old branch being cut off and thrown away. Notice how good you feel once you remove it. Now, emotionally reward yourself by celebrating that proud accomplishment in your heart.

11

Termites in Your Tree of Happiness

In my childhood, I heard of a mighty oak tree in my hometown. It was enormously tall with a broad trunk to give it an unshakable base. This vigorous tree withstood the most severe storms, strong winds, droughts, and even a grass fire. It seemed no force of nature could bring down this great oak.

However, one day, it eventually fell. And it fell to a moderate summer wind of all things. The wind was not that strong. How could it topple such a mighty oak? At first, people could not understand it. They gathered around the tree and mourned their losses; some even cried.

When the citizens examined the fallen tree more closely, they discovered an infestation of termites. Everyone was dumbfounded. Some tiny insects had destroyed such a robust structure. This towering tree admired by so many now lay on the ground, leveled by the persistent gnawing of pests that had worn it down over time.

Metaphorically, the same thing can happen to your serenity. Are there termites in your tree of happiness? If so, what exactly are those termites—domestic squabbles, work stress, congested traffic, unavailable parking, running late, and not having all the money you desire? What are the little irritations grinding you down and taking away your happiness? Isn't it interesting how these constant aggravations can slowly pick away at your tranquility? They may seem petty at the time, which could be why you ignore them at first. But in the long run, they eat your inner peace like termites.

People have their specific ideas of what happiness means to them. Some think certain events or special conditions must occur before happiness is possible. Maybe it is a precise income level, car, house, and so on. For them, contentment is only in the future, not the present.

Some adolescents don't think they can be happy until they leave their parents' house. Conversely, some parents say they won't be happy until their teenagers move out. College students look forward to graduation so they can finally be happy. Many childless couples believe they cannot be happy until they are married and have kids. Older working adults typically say they will finally be happy after retiring.

Why do we postpone joy? Time is flying by; today will never come again. Each moment is precious. Can we afford to wait? Sometimes, our definition of happiness is so narrow that we dismiss any pleasantness outside that definition. We should remove these maladaptive requirements, which we implement as preconditions to our happiness. To state it plainly, self-imposed restrictions on satisfaction are counterproductive. As an alternative, we can be content right now! There are many pathways to happiness, so don't listen to those who say there is only one way.

Have you considered that, for the most part, happiness is a decision? Well, now you have something new to think about. You can be happy in the present moment, whatever your circumstances. A decision like this does not have to be viewed as selfish because it is not just for you. Your joy benefits others, such as your family, coworkers, neighbors, and so on. When you are cheerful, that energy radiates to those around you, adding to their happiness. Face it—a good mood is catching! It is like seeing a baby smile and giggle; it makes you do the same.

Stop running after pleasure. You do not have to chase happiness and inner peace. It already exists within you. You only need to connect with it. Long-term contentment doesn't come from outside yourself; you can look within. Sure, you can find short-term excitement in some external material thing. But that excitement is transient and does not lead to a stable state of tranquility.

So, how do you connect with your inner harmony and fend off the proverbial termites that threaten your tree of happiness? Well, genuine contentment is in whatever you are doing here and now. Each moment is precious, so you need to take pleasure in the present. You cannot live in the past, nor can you live in the future. The only time you ever have is now. Therefore, this exact moment is the most critical time in your life. Enjoy it!

Now that you know true happiness comes from within, understand that your potential growth is within you, too. You already have what it takes to reach your potential. You have the aptitude to become the person you were born to be. Your true self lies dormant deep inside of you. All you need to do is be authentic.

Today's Teaching from Mother Nature

Having learned how to tap the waters of your inner happiness, it is now time to share that pleasure with others. All people have the potential for joy, and you can help them find it. Encourage contentment in those around you by being attentive to their emotional needs. Be like the giggling baby; let your smile be infectious until it spreads to everyone around you. It is a pleasure to be with you when you are joyful.

You cannot fake happiness. It will look contrived if you wear a false smile and pretend to be joyful. Let your cheerfulness flow from you like a fresh spring-fed mountain stream. There is no need to force it. You need to tap into the wells of your happiness before you can help others drill for their reservoirs. Then, not only will you understand how to repel the termites of negativity in your tree of happiness, but you will also be better able to teach others how to do the same for themselves.

12 Our Minds Circle Like an Eagle

A troubled mind can be full of ruminating thoughts about resentment, bitterness, anger, blame, and more. While driving my car one sunny morning, I saw a bald eagle flying high in the sky. At first, she looked like she had a clear destination in mind. To my surprise, the eagle turned and started circling as if focused on a small object on the ground. Something was occupying the eagle's mind that prevented her from going forward.

The repetitive circling of the eagle reminded me of the recurrent thoughts I sometimes have about unpleasant memories. Over the years, my mind keeps circling back to those hurts, time

and time again. Some of these memories are so trivial that they sound silly even to mention. For example, I recall reaching over the counter for a straw at a local ice cream shop as a child. The man behind the counter shouted at me, "Hey, kid! If you want a straw, ask for one!" When I tell this story, it doesn't sound so bad. I mean, it's not like he swore at me or anything. Yet, as a small child, I was startled by the loud voice and scared by the man's angry expression. Isn't it strange how my mind returns to that memory all these years later, like an eagle focused on something small and circling it?

One of the wisest lessons I have ever learned is to let go of past grievances. Otherwise, these ruminating thoughts can distract me from fully enjoying life today. I journal about some of my strongest positive and negative memories to put past issues to rest. I make sure I write down what I learned from each memory. That way, I grow from the experience as a plant does in the garden. Reviewing my life lessons can reveal a wealth of wisdom about myself. It allows me to look at things from a more constructive perspective.

You cannot completely heal past hurts without forgiving the offender. Yet, you cannot forgive someone without first having judged them. Did you realize that judgment comes before forgiveness? So, if you say you forgive someone, you judge them guilty of some offense first because forgiveness would not be necessary if there were no offenses. Furthermore, criticism is a form of judgment, too. If you are criticizing someone, you believe that person did something wrong. And that's a judgment.

Nearly everyone makes snap judgments from time to time. It's almost automatic. It does no good to feel ashamed because the shame then becomes a form of self-judgment. The trick is to become more aware of the times when we first start making these judgments so we can stop and forgive. We can't expect never to judge anyone ever again. Instead, we can try to minimize the time we spend ruminating on those offenses. Stopping and refusing to let our minds go on judging someone is automatic forgiveness. In that way, we let go of the resentment, and the healing begins.

While I'm on the topic of letting go, a while back, when I was fishing, I caught a catfish that was not even hooked. Why? Because the fish was hanging on to the hook with clamped jaws and would not let go. I was amazed at the stubbornness of that fish. Then, when I reeled the fish onto the shore and carefully pried the mouth open with my fingers, the hook just fell out! I practice catch-and-release, so after I gently put the fish back into the water, I kept thinking how stupid that fish was for not letting go earlier. All that struggle could have been avoided.

Then, it dawned on me. I sometimes act like that catfish when I refuse to let go of past hurts. I keep hanging on to bitterness and anger even though I understand that I will suffer less if I release the attachment I have to my animosity. But instead, my cynical mind keeps circling like an eagle.

Sometimes, it's not resentment troubling my mind—it's fear. These fears are not always based on reality; they often are figments of my imagination. Such was the case one morning when I was jogging down a gravel road in the country. From a side view, I thought I saw a gigantic bird sitting on the powerline half a block away. I could not quite distinguish what type of bird it was because it was so far away and looked so elongated. It appeared to be about six to seven feet long! This alarmed and confused me because I realized no birds in this area were that big.

I was shocked that some pieces from the middle of the alleged giant bird started to fly away. Then, parts from the end seemed to take flight. I was starting to freak out! I finally realized this was not just *one* large bird but roughly three dozen small birds sitting together on the line. Viewed from the side, they looked like one long bird. When I approached the small flock, it flew off in a flurry of flapping feathers.

That day, I discovered that not all my fears are what they seem at first. Once more, my troubled mind was afraid unnecessarily. I also learned that I need to replace my dysfunctional thinking patterns with more rational ones. Removing my negative thoughts is analogous to pulling weeds from a garden. Like weeds that grow up and block out the sun, hindering the desirable plants from growing, my fears also choke out the more desirable thoughts.

Today's Teaching from Mother Nature

What painful memories do you have circling like an eagle in your mind? Are there some people toward whom you are still harboring resentment? If you ignore the problem, the bitterness will grow like weeds. So, you have a choice: Either remove your mental weeds while they are still small, or let them grow tall and ruin your peace of mind. You decide. What do you think is the wisest decision?

13
A Dam of Bitterness Stops the Flow

People who persistently irritate you can cause you to feel resentment toward them. This includes self-serving politicians, employers who put profits before people, friends who don't return messages, noisy neighbors, an emotionally distant romantic partner, or fill in the blank. These resentments, over time, can cause a dam in your flow of positive energy and interfere with your ability to show kindness to others.

In nature, a beaver dam causes fresh water to back up, and the lack of flow results in the water turning stagnant over time. This blockage of fresh energy is analogous to people with dysfunctional behaviors, such as addiction or domestic abuse, to name only a few, which cause their home environments to become polluted with toxic energy. Usually, game fish will not stay in the stagnant water of a beaver dam because the lack of flow means insufficient fresh oxygen in the water for the fish to survive. Likewise, a mentally healthy person will not want to be around someone who has a poisonous personality because that type of personality is an emotional dam that blocks the flow of happiness.

So, what blocks your happiness? Perhaps it's from hurt feelings stemming from a recent argument, disappointments with a romantic partner, disturbing memories from childhood, or something else. Ultimately, a lack of *forgiveness* leads to a lack of *happiness*. Perhaps as a child, some bully said something hurtful to you, and now, all these years later, you are still hanging on to that resentment. It might ease your suffering to understand that the people who hurt you are emotionally wounded. In that way, they are like a black hole in outer space.

Allow me to elaborate. A black hole starts as a bright star, just as each person begins as an innocent baby. Then, something happens to the star, causing it to collapse upon itself to the point that the gravitational pull is so strong, it does not give anything back, not even light (hence the name, *black hole*). Similarly, people can get so emotionally wounded that they become self-centered and don't give anything back, not even love. People like this need our compassion, not our resentment.

Do your negative thoughts lead to feelings of bitterness, thoughts of criticism about a coworker, wishing the past would have turned out differently, wanting people to change to suit your needs, and so on? Maybe you wrecked your favorite car and couldn't stop wishing the accident never happened. Perhaps you ruminated on thoughts about the vehicle, such as thinking that if only you'd left your house at a different time and driven a different route, you would not have been in that accident.

When you experience a challenging event, do you find something positive or perceive it as negative and develop resentment? Let's say a member of your family, Goddess forbid, unexpectedly died! Could you see beyond your sorrow and pain to comfort those around you? Could you view the situation as an opportunity to show compassion to your grieving family? Or would your thoughts turn bitter as you focused on your hurt and how unfair it was that someone you loved had died? Each resentful thought is another log in the dam that blocks your happiness.

What if you accept the reality that nothing in life is permanent? Every living thing eventually alters into something else. Once you understand that even the ones you love will gradually change, you begin to accept that the transformation from one form into another is nature's way. With this level of understanding and acceptance of reality, it is unnecessary to suffer needlessly by wishing loved ones could stay the same forever.

With this type of mindset, you minimize the mourning process by accepting the fact that not even family members are going to be with you indefinitely. Then, you can focus on feeling grateful for the time that you *did* have to spend with that special person who passed. Furthermore, you can learn a valuable life lesson to not take people for granted; you never know how much time you have left with them.

Let's face it—we all have negative thoughts occasionally. We can't completely prevent all disturbing thoughts from popping into our heads. However, we don't need to entertain those thoughts by continually thinking about them and letting them upset us to the point that they become logs of resentment in our emotional dams. We don't have to review those past hurts in our minds repeatedly. After all, we can't change the past; we can only learn from it.

Okay, let's get practical. How can we let go of these feelings of resentment? How can we keep the positive energy flowing in our lives and minimize the logjams of bitterness? Learn to forgive. That's the main thing. Forgiveness prevents irritations and offenses from blocking the flow of kindness and love. Please understand that forgiveness does not mean that the other person's inappropriate actions are acceptable. Forgiveness involves letting go of the anger and hurt in your heart; it does not excuse the injurious offense.

Instead of harboring resentment, you can turn those counterproductive thoughts into thoughts about caring for and protecting vulnerable people. This topic reminds me of a pair of hawks I saw years ago. The female hawk was vulnerable because she perched to feed on a lower branch near the ground. On a higher branch, the male hawk was protecting his mate by periodically screeching to warn predators to stay away.

We, too, can be like that guardian hawk. We can protect and watch out for each other. We can render aid when seeing a person on the street in a vulnerable situation. At work, if someone speaks disrespectfully to a coworker, we can remind everyone that we are a team that needs to support one another. Moreover, at home, we can be more sensitive to the vulnerable feelings of our family members.

Today's Teaching from Mother Nature

It's time to release those logs of resentment that block the flow of happiness and break apart the mental dams we have in our minds. Let's wash away that stagnant water by opening the stream of loving energy in our hearts so we can better ease the suffering of others with our compassion and understanding.

14
Nurture Yourself Like the Snowy Owl

Sometimes, we get so caught up in our negative thoughts and memories that it is hard to focus on enjoying what's happening right now. Setting those damaging thoughts aside is a form of self-nurturing. Our higher consciousness often communicates meaningful information to us in our dreams. This information can guide us to navigate the maze of life.

I experienced such a dream. Before bed that night, I pondered how to best deal with my distressing memories. Those troublesome thoughts kept creeping into my mind and robbing me of the gift of now. Then, after falling asleep, I dreamed of walking into my house to

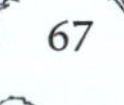

find several dogs and cats that didn't belong to me. I didn't want them in my home, but I also didn't want them outside where they might get lost. I was concerned about their well-being and put them on the porch with food and water.

After the pets were safe on the porch, I thoroughly walked through my house. It looked as though someone had robbed me, and I wanted to make sure the burglar was no longer there. I searched the house but did not find any intruders. However, my house looked ransacked with things scattered on the floor.

After I woke up, I thought about the meaning of this dream. My higher self soon revealed that the dogs and cats represented hurtful memories from my past. The rooms in the house represented the areas in my mind where memories reside. As it turns out, the animals were the ones who had made a mess of the place. Whatever they could reach, they'd pulled down from the shelves onto the floor. The items on the higher shelves represented my higher conscious mind, and those things were undisturbed.

The message I gleaned from this was that these disturbing memories were ransacking the rooms in my mind. I needed to nurture myself by putting those negative memories out on the porch and not focusing on them so much. It's not that I must put them entirely out of my mind; however, I don't need to cling to those memories, either. That's why, in my dream, I didn't put the animals outside; I was not trying to get rid of them completely.

Whenever I think about one of those intrusive memories now, I order that memory out to the porch. This mental exercise makes me smile and sometimes laugh, which is far better than feeling bad. That's self-nurturing!

Instead of resenting the people from my past who offended me, I can mentally send them to the porch. Then, those negative thoughts don't rob my mind from enjoying life here and now. Besides, I can't change the past. What good does it do to rehash painful memories?

There are countless ways to self-nurture and be fully present in life. One of the simplest ways is to take a slow, deep breath while thinking about how the fresh oxygen nourishes the cells in your body. Then, as you exhale, think about being kind to people. Breathe in for yourself and breathe out for others.

The subject of self-nurturing reminds me of a snowy owl I witnessed descending from a light pole and diving into the snow to capture some prey. After the snowy owl flew off, I mentally asked the majestic creature if she had a message. What immediately popped into my head was that the owl was modeling behavior for me. The message was found in what the owl was doing—feeding and nurturing itself. And I need to do the same. I need to practice more awareness of how I care for myself, body, mind, and spirit. I can start nurturing my emotional health by dismissing counterproductive thoughts and memories.

So how about you? Do you have any memories that trouble you? If you do, perhaps you can put those negative thoughts in their place by ordering them out to the proverbial porch. Nurture yourself with a cleansing breath, and upon exhalation, think about forgiving the person who hurt you in the past without excusing that person's negative behavior. This practice may take some time. Letting go of a painful memory does not always happen overnight; it could take months or years. Be patient with yourself.

Additionally, you are not expected to let go of all negative thoughts. However, you can learn to shorten the time you spend thinking about those painful memories. That leaves you more time to appreciate life today.

What else can you do to nurture yourself? Along with eating healthy nutrients, you may also want to consider feeding your mind healthier messages. Banishing hurtful memories onto the proverbial porch is a good start. However, what about banning the negative media messages around you that cause suffering? These manipulative messages could include advertisements designed to make you feel incomplete because you don't have the products they sell.

What about banishing the negative energy produced by destructive emotions such as hatred, resentment, bitterness, jealousy, and the like? Or what about setting some healthy limits so that you do not spend so much time in the company of people who radiate toxic energy because they destructively express their negative emotions?

Today's Teaching from Mother Nature

Whenever poisonous memories creep into your mind, breathe in for yourself and breathe out for the people who hurt you. Follow the example of the snowy owl and take care of yourself. Your breath nurtures you and helps keep you mindful of the present moment. Then, you are not robbed of the gift of enjoying the life experience that is currently happening.

15
Hurt People Can Be Like Vicious Animals

When dealing with angry people, remember that behind the anger is usually a lot of fear and hurt. They may be afraid something will go wrong or that they will look foolish or lose something or someone. However, in most cases, their anger is a mask hiding some emotional injury. Remember, an injured animal is a vicious animal. Similarly, some people (not all) who are suffering might exhibit misplaced anger as a defense mechanism and inappropriately lash out at those around them.

What if you had a blatantly hostile supervisor? Reminiscent of an injured animal, she was vicious in every way. Her words were cutting and could hurt just as deeply as the claws of a frightened, wild animal. Moreover, she could sense others' vulnerabilities and exploit their weaknesses. In many ways, her behavior resembles a predator stalking its prey.

There is a valuable lesson to be learned from this theoretical example—vulnerability attracts predators. When wolves smell blood or see a wounded animal, they move in for the kill. And, yes, some humans, too, develop a predatory personality along with the accompanying sociopathic behavior.

My point? Don't let your vulnerabilities show around people acting hostile or otherwise displaying antisocial behavior. If you want an example, think of your ex! Remember how your former partner used to prey upon your weakness. You found out too late that sharing your vulnerable side was later used against you in an argument or, worse, in a divorce court! Your ex exploited your tender feelings and personal stories by springing that personal information on you in the form of a verbal ambush.

If you have ever dated someone who preyed upon your vulnerabilities, you know that whenever you apologized, your partner began criticizing you even more. You quickly discovered that the more you apologized, the more you were verbally attacked. It was as if your mate interpreted your apologizing as a weakness and moved in for the kill. This is classic predatory behavior! No wonder you felt on edge during that relationship. If you think back, you may recall how your subconscious manifested those negative emotions into disturbing dreams. What were your dreams like when you were going through your breakup?

While I was in a dysfunctional same-sex relationship, I had a nightmare that involved me taking a group tour at the top of a skyscraper. I got distracted and fell behind the group. Then, someone snuck up behind me and threw me over the railing to my death. The lesson I learned from that cautionary dream was not to turn my back on someone dangerous because I might get seriously hurt or killed.

I also learned to stick with the group and not isolate myself. There's safety in numbers. That's why predators try to separate their would-be prey from the herd. They want their target to be vulnerable. That nightmare taught me not to be so naive.

One night, I witnessed an example of vulnerability when I saw an owl dive into traffic and get killed. The owl fixated on the mouse running across the road so much that he did not see the traffic. The owl was vulnerable because he had tunnel vision. That's not to say, of course, that the owl does not have any positive qualities. Can you see yourself in this owl? Has there ever been a time when you got so wrapped up in what you were doing that you did not see trouble approaching, like letting bills pile up, maybe?

All mammals, including humans, have strengths and weaknesses. I saw the strength of the red-tailed hawk on a sunny afternoon. I watched her dive into a ditch to get her prey. The message I gleaned from that experience was to seize the moment and strike opportunities quickly without delay. Can you see yourself in this hawk? Can you answer the door when opportunity knocks, or do you hesitate until the moment is gone? When did you last take a calculated risk and pursue your goal wholeheartedly? If you had a momentary setback, did you keep trying until you succeeded?

One night, I thought about the behavioral differences between the owl and the hawk. The owl has night vision, allowing him to zoom in and focus on what he is seeing. His brain blocks out all other distractions, which can be beneficial under certain circumstances. Unfortunately, the owl can also become so narrowly focused that he does not see approaching danger.

On the other hand, the hawk has the gift of broader vision. By soaring high in the sky, she can look far to the horizon, view the whole scene, and anticipate danger. The drawback is that seeing the big picture can cause the hawk to become easily distracted by all the commotion in the scene.

Today's Teaching from Mother Nature

Lowering your guard when you are with someone you trust is okay. However, don't be vulnerable when there is danger nearby. Watch out for that owllike tunnel vision so you don't get blindsided by people full of rage. Having compassion for people who are hurting does not mean leaving yourself vulnerable to being mistreated. To be clear, not everyone who is suffering is going to lash out like an injured animal. Still, it is wise to practice some protection and self-care. Therefore, look around and be aware of your surroundings.

Learn from both the owl and the hawk. Focus on the present moment like the owl while watching for oncoming danger. When showing compassion for others' suffering, keep a broad view like the hawk without being distracted by all the chaos around you.

16
The Tree of Deep-Rooted Relations

Are you looking for a romantic partner to rescue you from your unhappiness? Do you believe that your happiness is in the hands of someone else? I can't tell you how many times I have heard people of all genders and sexual orientations speak of finding someone to make them happy, as if happiness lies outside of themselves.

Expecting another person to bring you happiness can be a dilemma. However, there is a way out of this quandary—be content with yourself as you are. When you are at peace with yourself, you can be at peace with those around you. That type of inner peace is the root that can anchor any relationship and provide stability. Then, you may not feel as much need to be rescued by a romantic partner or that cute face you see across the bar after you've chugged the last of your beer. (Hiccup!)

There is a large weeping willow in my front yard, and I often think about how the characteristics of that tree compare to a romantic relationship. For one thing, flexibility is essential. The tree needs to bend when the strong winds blow. I recall looking out the window during one of those ferocious thunderstorms that shook the whole house. I watched the upper branches of that weeping willow whip from side to side like streamers. Despite the chaotic gyrations of the upper branches, the tree had a strong trunk with deep roots that gave it stability.

So, what are the foundational roots of *your* relationships? Have you taken the time to develop relational roots yet? Some individuals go through romantic partners so quickly that they do not give themselves the time necessary to establish those roots. You really can't commit to a relationship without some foundation. Ask yourself what the relationship is based on. Do both you and your partner agree with the answers? Have you even talked about it?

Before you talk to your partner about commitment, carefully consider whether your words will help or hurt. Your relationship may not be at the point where talking about commitment is necessary yet. If the two of you are starting to get to know each other, one way to determine your partner's level of commitment is to see how well promises are kept. This simple personality trait is at the heart of a relational foundation because it deals with trust and can often be detected surprisingly early on.

Admittedly, sometimes, a person cannot help but break a promise once in a blue moon. However, if your partner has never kept even one promise, please pardon my bluntness when I wonder why you are still together. (I mean, really?!) That's called denial. You can only ignore the problem for so long.

Okay, back to the tree analogy. The weeping willow is also nurturing. It gives off oxygen and provides a protective habitat for nesting birds. Additionally, the tree is part of a larger community of trees. It is beautiful by itself without competing with others. Likewise, a caring attitude can improve all your relationships, romantic or otherwise. Listening is one of the best ways to show you care. Keep in mind that genuine care is reciprocal. Any functional relationship needs a sense of balance and equality. If a problem needs to be resolved, talk to your partner when you are calm. Learn how to work out conflicts with a win-win style to satisfy both of you.

Remember, your life partner cannot meet all your emotional and social needs. Trees have the forest community. Likewise, you need friends and community involvement outside your primary relationship. It is too much to expect your partner to be your everything. Technically, your partner cannot make you happy. Only you can foster long-term happiness within yourself. No one else can do it for you. Your partner is not there to save you from your unpleasant emotions.

In many counseling sessions, I listened to clients express unrealistic expectations about their romantic partners. The expectations ranged from blaming their partners for all their unhappiness to demanding that their partners make them happy immediately. Those are the types of counterproductive comments made by people who, quite frankly, did not want to take responsibility for their feelings. They didn't need rescuing; they needed to change their codependent attitudes! (There, I said it. Well, somebody had to.)

Today's Teaching from Mother Nature

As with the weeping willow, when relational storms come along, bend but don't break. Be flexible and adapt to the inevitable changes that come with life. With an open-minded perspective, you can accept that everything grows and transforms over time. The tree adapts to change while still nurturing. So can you.

17
The Fearful Dog and Scared Rabbit

We all feel afraid sometimes. However, did you realize that fear happens when your mind predicts a negative outcome? Things we don't understand can appear threatening at first. An upcoming meeting with the boss, a blind date, waiting to get lab results back from the physician, or meeting a stranger can all seem intimidating. The list goes on and on. It is not until we gather more information about a given situation that we can put our fears aside and make an informed decision rather than an emotional reaction or snap judgment.

This fearful mindset always reminds me of something I once saw my dog do. I was planting a tree in my backyard and dug a large hole. Alongside the hole was a big mound of dirt with grass clumps sticking out. My dog was advanced in years and had cataracts, which prevented clear vision. When my dog trotted around the corner of the house to the backyard, she took one look at that pile of dirt and immediately started to growl. The fur on her shoulders and rump went up in a defensive posture because she mistakenly thought it was a predator.

It wasn't until she slowly got close enough to smell the dirt that she realized the grassy pile was not a furry animal threatening her. I swear she looked embarrassed! The lesson I learned from my dog that day was not to assume something is threatening until it is checked out first.

Let's look at a fictional character, Cassondra, who was in a similar situation to the fearful dog example. Her anxiety was interfering with her ability to make a sound decision. Her boyfriend asked Cassondra if she wanted to move in with him. He told her he would buy her a new car if she did, and she needed reliable transportation. The only catch is that he and Cassondra had different religions, and he disagreed with her beliefs. She feared they might not get along if she moved in with him. And if they didn't get along, they might break up. She knew several couples who had broken up after they'd started living together. So, she wasn't sure if moving in was a good idea.

As you can imagine, this decision was difficult for Cassondra because she did not know what her boyfriend would do. Maybe he had a hidden agenda, such as wanting to convert her to his religious way of thinking. On the other hand, perhaps he didn't. She couldn't decide what to do and kept going back and forth like a jittery rabbit running this way and that. The trouble with a jittery rabbit is that the zigzagging movement it makes when it is nervous attracts unwanted attention from predators. The more fearful the rabbit gets, the more peril it draws to itself.

Many couples of mixed religious backgrounds have found common ground and compromised to stay together and continue their relationship. However, Cassondra's boyfriend already indicated that he disagreed with her spirituality. Therefore, the topic of faith was a point of contention between the two of them. But it doesn't have to be. It all depends on how willing the couple is to compromise and find common ground. The big question is how committed they are to making their relationship work.

Tell me, was there something that bothered you about Cassondra's boyfriend offering to purchase a car for her as a term for her agreeing to move in? Doesn't it sound like he was offering incentives to sweeten the pot? I understand that romantic partners often buy gifts for their sweethearts, but the context of this situation is different. Cassondra's partner seemed to be trying to lure her in. I don't like that feeling at all. How about you?

Remember that if he can offer her incentives, he can take them away or stop buying her things. She would, essentially, owe him a huge favor or emotional debt. Does that sound like an equal relationship? I can see where that might lead to some feelings of resentment down the road, especially if he expects something from her in return. He might try to get her to join him in church activities. Maybe his church accepts people of different faiths. We don't know. It sounds risky. No wonder Cassondra was as jittery as a rabbit.

So, is her nervousness attracting more problems? In other words, is her fearfulness making things in the relationship worse? Well, that all depends on whether the perceived threat is real. Is that suspicious mound on the lawn a dangerous animal or just a clump of dirt with grass sticking out? Who knows? In Cassondra's fictional situation, let's assume she knows her boyfriend well enough to rely on her intuition to determine whether the threat is real.

If you could talk to Cassondra, what suggestions would you have for her? Might you advise her to sit down with her partner and talk heart-to-heart? She can have a list of questions to ask him and things she wants to tell him about herself. She needs to tell him how she feels about his nonacceptance of her spirituality and about her concerns regarding the problems that might develop if the two of them live under the same roof. Asking him directly if he can accept her as she is without trying to change her is most likely the best way to determine if her fear is bona fide. Cassondra also needs to be just as direct with him about whether she can accept *him*. It works both ways.

Today's Teaching from Mother Nature

Here's the summary, short and sweet: Before allowing your mind to imagine the worst, find out whether the threat is real. It's that simple.

18
Are You a Timid Turkey or a Brave Bird?

What would you say if you knew a college student who sought your counsel regarding whether to pursue his career interest or follow the path his father had laid out for him? Let's play this scene out in our imagination. What if this young man said he wanted to enter the workforce immediately, but his dad told him he should first go to college for four years? Assume that the son doesn't know what to do and is afraid to make a mistake he will regret for the rest of his life. What would you say to this young man?

Since the young man expressed a strong interest in starting his own business, you might advise him to communicate that message clearly to his father. The son needs to concentrate on what he wants in life rather than on what the father wants for the son's life. The young person seemed so scared of making a mistake that it was as though he was focused more on what he feared would happen rather than on succeeding in his endeavors.

I understand how making major life decisions can be difficult. I sit quietly and clear my mind when I make a crucial choice. I focus on who I am at my core. What is the essence of my being? What is my true nature? Understanding the answers to these questions means understanding my path in life. Then, everything seems more straightforward, and I can decide what to do.

Please keep in mind that any lifepath can change as time passes. The person you are today is not exactly who you will be in ten years. Nothing stays precisely the same. That's the thing about lifepaths; they keep turning in new directions. What starts as a straight road can suddenly veer sharply to the left or right. Then, boom! You have a new heading and are on another course, hopefully for the better. That is why it is so important to adapt to life changes. If you don't adapt, you don't function very well.

Perhaps this concept can be best illustrated by a real-life example I saw in nature. While driving down a country road, I saw a turkey standing alone at the edge of the woods. Then, I saw several other turkeys about thirty yards away eating seeds in the open field. The lone turkey would not leave the safety of the woods to step into the field because of the risk of being exposed to predators.

I learned from this observation that I need to leave my comfort zone and venture out with calculated risk to get what I want in life. Let me plainly state that taking a calculated risk does not mean being reckless. It means measuring the costs and being willing to face the consequences if things turn ugly. It has been my experience that deciding to take a calculated risk has far more rewards than losses.

That is how I decided years ago to go to college; I weighed the pros and cons and took a calculated risk. I struggle with a learning disability called dyslexia, so I was not sure if I could manage the scholastic demands of college life, especially in the areas of math and reading. In high school, an academic advisor told me I should not go to college because he didn't think I could handle all that required reading.

As a result of that misguided advice, I did not go to college for the first two years after high school. I worked the night shift on an assembly line in a paper factory. It was not until I overcame my fears that I dared to enroll in college. I am not saying that I ignored my fears completely. I do listen to my fears because they can warn me of real danger. However, I do not let fear run my life because, all too often, the threat is not real at all, just paranoia. I think of it this way: My life journey is like a car ride, and I let the fear ride in the back seat but never let it take the steering wheel.

I weighed the costs and benefits. The emotional cost for me to keep working on the night shift assembly line was so undesirable that I used that distress as motivation to go to college. Like the turkeys in the field, I was finally ready to step into the open to get what I wanted. I had to take the risk of failing before I could have a chance of reaping the rewards of success. And succeed, I did. Once I had proper accommodation from the school for my learning disability (or, as I like to call it, my *alternative learning style*), I started earning high grades and made the dean's list within the first year. I continued to succeed academically with tutoring assistance until I completed my doctorate.

Today's Teaching from Mother Nature

What lessons did you learn from those turkeys? Do you want to stay in the safety of the woods or venture out into the open? Do you want to follow the advice of timid people and be more secure with a seemingly safer lifestyle, or do you want to take the riskier route and forge a custom lifepath for yourself? In other words, what type of turkey are you?

19

How Ravens Taught Me About Friendship

I found that if I do not reach out first to new people, they usually do not take the initiative to reach out to me. Therefore, it is up to me to introduce myself and form the beginnings of a friendship. This idea of giving before receiving is a lesson the ravens taught me.

I treated ravens with aloofness for years, mostly because I witnessed ravens pestering and even attacking owls during daylight hours. Since owls are special to me in a spiritual way, I tend to defend them. So, it seemed only natural for me to dislike ravens. When I saw ravens in my yard, I used to wave my arms over my head and scare them away.

It did not take long for the ravens to begin disliking me. Pretty soon, all I had to do was leave the house, and the ravens would start to squawk as quickly as they saw me. It appeared we had become enemies. Now what? Is that the type of relationship I wanted with these birds? No, it wasn't. That's when I realized that I needed to do something to improve the situation.

I stopped chasing them out of my yard, but to my surprise, it did little to improve things. They still squawked whenever they saw me. This behavior went on for several months. Then, shortly after the first snowfall of the year, I started thinking about how the food sources for the ravens diminished during the winter months. So, I began putting out some dry bread for the ravens to eat, which they did eagerly. And that is when their reaction toward me started to change.

In the weeks and months that followed, the ravens stopped sounding a warning call when they spotted me. Instead, when I walked outside, they watched me with anticipation of more food. Now, they treat me like a welcome friend, the kind of friend who always brings a tasty dish over to the house for social occasions.

After learning this life lesson of giving first before receiving, I incorporated that wisdom into my life. For example, when I moved to a new town, I didn't wait for the neighbors to come over to introduce themselves. On the contrary, I approached *them*, knocking on doors and shaking hands.

I did not know how friendly my new neighbors were, so walking up to their houses and introducing myself was challenging for an introverted gay guy like me.

How did I do it? After some contemplation, I decided to bake a nice batch of fudge-chunk cookies to bring to all the neighbors as a friendly gesture. It was fun making the cookies and imagining the expressions on their faces when they opened the door and saw my shiny face smiling over a plate of freshly baked cookies. I wondered how they might respond. I tried to keep my predictions positive. It was easy to be optimistic about the outcome because who can resist the soft, gooey goodness of homemade cookies still warm from the oven? I admit, it was a type of seduction. Well, sort of. (You know what I mean.)

So, I stood before the steps of the first neighbor's house and rang the doorbell. A few moments later, the door swung open. Standing before me was a large, angry-looking, burly man with a lot of facial hair wearing a sleeveless white undershirt and an expression that told me I was disturbing him. At first, I was tempted to drop the plate of cookies and run away screaming, leaving a cloud of pixie dust in my wake. But then, I thought if I did that, it would only reinforce negative stereotypes of people who are gay like me. So, I abandoned my thoughts of fleeing and stood steady.

With a fixed grin, I introduced myself and held out the tasty peace offering I'd baked. The man invited me inside, and after a polite visit, we quickly became friends. He told me that I was welcome at his house anytime. Thus, a new friendship was born by following the lessons taught by the ravens.

Today's Teaching from Mother Nature

Perhaps you, too, can learn a lesson from the ravens in this story: Make sure you reach out to new people instead of waiting for them to make the first move. It is too easy to sit back and passively observe people. It can be tempting to think that if others want to talk, they should approach first. But it is not enough to be patient and wait until others make the first move because if you overcome your trepidations, you can make new friends sooner.

Just like I made a friendly gesture to the ravens by offering them food, you can offer a stranger a smile and a friendly handshake. Take the initiative and introduce yourself. It takes courage because most people feel a little anxious when striking up a conversation with a new person. But you may discover that the other person feels just as nervous as you do. There you go; now you have something in common.

20
Turning a New Leaf in Relationships

During springtime a few years ago, I was walking through the woods, enjoying the earthy smell of the wet soil and the sweet scent of new blossoms. Spring has always symbolized a time for turning over a new leaf and starting over. Although this concept can take many forms, it may also indicate a need to move on and disconnect from dysfunctional relationships.

So, what constitutes a dysfunctional relationship? Well, for one thing, any relationship becomes dysfunctional at the point where the dynamics of that relationship interfere with personal growth. For example, you might have a long-term romantic partner who meets some of your needs, yet you feel bored. Things are not exactly bad. It's just that you are only somewhat content with the status quo. The two of you have a routine, and it's becoming uncomfortable because things are always the same from one day to the next. In other words, the relationship is too predictable.

So, what's the problem, you ask? The problem is that there's little to no personal growth because you are both in a rut. There is nothing inherently wrong with being somewhat content and having a routine in your relationship. But, when the predictability lulls you into a state of cognitive slumber, it neutralizes your motivation to further develop and grow as a couple.

Of course, this does not mean you must break up with your partner. It does, however, mean that you need to find some way to bring new life and energy into the relationship; call it a renewal. The two of you can turn over a new leaf by starting a project together, going to a couples retreat, finding a new hobby, getting in shape, or taking a class that you both enjoy.

Perhaps this renewal concept needs a brief story for clarification. One day, I was hiking in the woods and came across a tiny pine sapling. It grew from the composting stump of an old, rotted pine tree that had died years ago. I looked at this scene, thinking that if a seed could take root and grow out of the remains of a dead tree, then perhaps I could sprout a new leaf from the old skeletons in my closet of life.

This concept can apply to any aspect of your life and any relationship. Take, for example, your relationship with your family of origin. If you are an adult living independently, look closely at the quality of your relationships with your family members. Do they enhance your life? Do you enrich *their* lives? Do all your family members, including you, encourage each other to improve and grow as individuals? Do they have flexible boundaries for each member to follow their lifepath? These challenging questions need to be answered if you want to determine the functionality of these relationships.

Once you assess which family connections are healthy because they promote growth and which are unhealthy because they discourage self-improvement, you can decide which ones to spend your energy on and which to limit your contact with. This thought may sound harsh, but not every family member will have a compatible personality with yours. That's okay. No law states that all family members must like each other. Sometimes, personalities don't mix well together.

Let's manufacture a situation to illustrate this point. Imagine there is a friend of yours named Lisa who grew up in a rather large family. Furthermore, imagine your friend has always felt slightly different from her siblings and never quite fit in. Why? Let's chalk it up to personality differences; Lisa was more outgoing, freethinking, and nonconforming.

On the other hand, her brothers and sisters kept more to themselves, didn't question any preestablished rules, and were rigidly conventional.

So, is anyone wrong in this fictitious scenario? Of course not. People can live however they want, provided they do not injure anyone. So, what's the problem with Lisa? As an independent adult, she felt obligated to attend family functions even though she did not want to be around them. Her presence at these family gatherings caused tension and disharmony because of their differences.

They know she does not believe as they do; they know she has a more gregarious lifestyle than the rest. And that is what they saw in her each time she visited—a sister who strayed from family tradition. Like it or not, the fact is that there are social consequences for breaking away from the group and forging a new path as an individual. Can you relate?

After much contemplation, Lisa realized that not only did her siblings not accept her way of life, but she did not accept theirs. This revelation opened Lisa's eyes to a new point of view. Her brothers and sisters have a more peaceful and enjoyable time when she is not interacting with them.

It was hard for this fictional friend to face this new perspective at first, but when Lisa finally acknowledged that it was okay for siblings to go their separate ways and that she did not need to find fault with any of them, she was at peace with her decision and turned a new leaf. As a result, she limited the time she spent with her family, dramatically reducing the tension she was feeling. She can still attend a few family gatherings—not all of them, and not for long periods.

Today's Teaching from Mother Nature

Do you need to turn over a new leaf with some relationships in your life? Remember that this does not mean removing yourself from those relationships altogether. It just means you need to reassess them. Are those relationships still functional, and to what degree? It may be time to pull back the reins and conserve some of your energy for other things.

21

Removing Emotional Thorns

All too often, when I went out in the woods to connect with nature, I got stuck with thorns under my skin. Even after coming home, if I accidentally touched one of those thorns embedded in me, I felt the stinging pain. I wanted to avoid pain, so I tried removing the thorn immediately. As I dug out that nasty thorn, I realized negative memories could sting like thorns.

Do you try to avoid painful memories? Such uncomfortable recollections are like thorns under your skin. If you have a thorn, it is only natural to protect that sensitive area. Similarly, you also want to protect the places where hurtful memories reside to avoid evoking those thoughts.

The amount of wasted energy spent trying to avoid these painful memory thorns is shocking. We evade any plans or activities that might remind us of the hurt. At that point, avoidance becomes a central part of our lives. If the pain is severe enough, we may even terminate a relationship because our emotional thorns keep getting touched.

Remember, your attention goes to the most significant stimulus. In other words, you scratch the biggest itch. To put so much focus on your pain takes your awareness away from other, more pleasant experiences. For example, what if you had an insecure self-image and consequently chose a romantic partner primarily because that person flattered you and reinforced your ego? Can you see the thorn in this scenario and how it distracts your awareness? What painful issue are you trying to avoid? That's your thorn!

A few compliments exchanged between lovers are not harmful, of course. It can be healthy if balanced with other values. However, if receiving kudos is your primary reason for being with that person, you may want to look at your motives. Are you avoiding the pain of low self-esteem by seeking narcissistic validation like a strutting peacock fanning its colorful feathers to impress a mate?

Instead of trying to tiptoe around emotional pain, it's much healthier to lean into your hurt by facing it. Accept the reality of your situation and acknowledge the difficult emotions. You cannot deal with something if you do not believe it. And if you don't deal with it, the hurt will not disappear. Sometimes, time can heal emotional wounds, but that's assuming you deal with those emotions over time. You cannot overcome something by suppressing it and denying the problem exists.

Case in point: A distressing emotion is like cholesterol accumulating sticky plaque in your arteries. A little bit won't kill you, but if enough plaque builds up over time, you have significant problems. Your life-giving blood cannot pump through a blocked artery. Likewise, you cannot psychologically function at your best when you have an emotional blockage. You need to clean out those mental arteries so your life energy can flow freely again.

Such an emotional cleaning can be uncomfortable. Think of it this way—if those memories were full of strong emotions when you suppressed them deep inside, they would still be full of strength when you removed the lid. I don't think the unconscious mind has a sense of time. Therefore, your blocked emotions could be as fresh as the day you bottled them up.

Unfortunately, some of the people closest to you may know about your emotional thorns and, when angered, intentionally try to poke at them. It's a nasty thing to do, yet it happens. Take, for instance, an argument you are having with your romantic partner. Your partner gets mad and purposefully says something sure to hurt your feelings.

This type of thing can happen with family members, too. So, just be mindful that when people push your buttons, they poke your emotional thorns.

Today's Teaching from Mother Nature

The first step in dealing with emotional thorns is to raise your awareness and acknowledge you are afraid of getting hurt. In and of itself, avoiding pain is not a problem. It is only natural to dodge injuries. However, avoidant behavior becomes problematic when it interferes with life functioning. When you start to dodge people and stay away from places that remind you of your emotional thorns, you know your avoidant behavior is beginning to interfere with your life. In that case, you are not dealing with your fears. The problem with trying to sidestep your thorns is that you are not getting rid of them; they are still there.

Once you are mindful that you have an emotional thorn in your psyche, work on removing it before it festers. Do this by forgiving the people who hurt you, and remember to forgive yourself. Repeat this exercise of forgiveness every time your emotional thorn gets bumped and those painful memories return. Please note that we are only talking about memories from the past, not the present. If you have a situation where someone is currently causing you emotional harm, please get in touch with a professional counselor to help you find a constructive way to resolve the issue as soon as possible.

22

Puppies Fully Enjoy Life. Do You?

Watching puppies playing around with each other always makes me laugh. How about you? When you laugh, it not only makes *you* feel good, but it also makes the people *around* you laugh—then *they* feel good, too. That is because laughing is contagious. Maybe you've experienced a situation where somebody in the room got the giggles and couldn't stop laughing. That humorous mood spread throughout the group quickly, and everyone cracked up. Perhaps you noticed how all that shared laughter improved people's overall moods.

The fact that laughter improves your mood indicates that you don't laugh because you are *happy*, but rather, you are happy *because* you laugh. (Hmm?) Laughter can contribute to your happiness. If you feel down, try watching your favorite comedian, humorous movie, funny animal videos, or just spending time with jovial friends. You might find that humor can lift you out of a gloomy mood, at least briefly.

Keep in mind that laughter, like smiling, is a gift you give to others. There might be a time when someone you care about is feeling sad. That is the perfect opportunity to show compassion and utilize the gift of humor to help that person feel better. And why stop with just one person? You could share your sparkling wit with your family, roommates, and coworkers. If humor is appropriate to the situation and surroundings, you can do a tremendous favor to everyone by using laughter to raise the moods of those around you. Think of it as a comedy break.

You probably already know that laughter can reduce stress, right? One way to do that is to view stress differently to change your experience of the tension. Find something about the stressful situation that is humorous. Reframe your thoughts to change your perception. This can take the anxious edge off what is happening. In your mind, picture one aspect of the situation that is odd or weird. Then, see the absurdity in it. How strange is that? Go ahead and chuckle. Sometimes, life can be very bizarre. Oh, well.

As a word of caution, be sure when you make a joke, you use positive humor, not something that insults or puts down anyone. You intend to lighten the mood with humor, not make fun of people, groups, cultures, lifestyles, or beliefs.

Individuals moving toward a state of open-mindedness seem to be able to appreciate the abundance of incongruities that life has to offer. They can laugh at the mistakes they make without getting down on themselves. They keep things light with a playful and spontaneous nature. This type of well-rounded individual does not use sarcastic humor to hurt others. Sarcasm is hostile, plain and simple.

In romantic relationships, use non-injurious humor as a way of bonding. It can bring couples closer when they laugh together regularly. Most couples I've spoken to have said having a sense of humor is one of the most essential things in their relationship. Often, divorced people say that if they ever get married again, they will ensure their new spouse has a sense of humor. It's that important!

It is curious how jokes seem to have a basis in some truism. For example, when we joke about the ironies of life, we laugh because they are true. Life is full of absurdities, so why not enjoy the farce? We can all learn to laugh a little more. Not that we shouldn't take *anything* seriously. It's just that we shouldn't take *everything* so seriously. Plenty of issues and concerns in the world require our attention. However, humor and laughter can be handy tools for a temporary break from stress and problems.

Think of humor as a welcome respite from the storms of life. Isn't it true that we tend to laugh after a scary event has passed and it's all over? How often have we chuckled as we've wiped the sweat from our brows after a near miss or close call? We tend to laugh at our fears. In that way, humor can be a weapon against stress. Somehow, laughter keeps us from going to pieces.

Several years back, I did a little unofficial experiment on humor in the workplace. Before this social experiment, humor was always part of my regular communication style at any place I worked. However, I thought I would see what would happen if I did not use my sense of humor for three months. I stopped joking around, didn't laugh at the jokes of others, and didn't smile. I still got all my work done but without lightheartedness.

Well, the results were dramatic! Right away, I felt more stressed about every task I did. My coworkers seemed unusually tense as well. Perhaps they thought I felt depressed. When I stopped smiling at them, they quickly stopped smiling at me. I also noticed that they did not engage me in conversation as often as they had when I'd been my jovial self. Wow! What a considerable difference humor and laughter can make.

Today's Teaching from Mother Nature

Think about what your life would be like without laughter. It's not a pretty thought. Picture in your head those playful puppies enjoying life to the fullest. Now, make up your mind to laugh more often and be lighthearted. Decide to stop using offensive humor that can injure the feelings of others and instead embrace the positive humor that enhances life. Share the gift of laughter with your loved ones and see how it improves your relationships.

23

Deer Do Not Assume Anything

Beliefs and opinions need to be updated and challenged over time. Your point of view is just your perception of things, not the absolute truth. Think back ten years. Didn't you have beliefs that now seem unfounded, even irrational? At the time, you were pretty sure you were right. However, knowing what you know now, you would never hold those same outdated beliefs again. In your early childhood, perhaps you thought you were born to be an astronaut or ballet dancer, only to lose interest in those things a few years later.

Don't be like the proverbial farm animals that, in panic, run back into the burning barn!

Perhaps you've heard those stories about how livestock are driven out of a burning barn, and then, not knowing what to do, the animals rely on their familiar habits and charge right back into the barn with flames leaping out of the doors. The animals want to go to a safe place to seek protection. Yet, the old routine is no longer secure. Things have changed; therefore, not checking to see if the old beliefs remain true leads them to a deadly mistake. It's all about false assumptions. The outdated thought patterns may not reflect the reality of the current situation.

What if you take a lesson from the watchful deer instead of assuming your old beliefs are correct? When deer enter a new situation, they enter cautiously. They do not just assume that they are safe to go ahead unthinkingly. Each step is chosen vigilantly, and each scene is questioned. The deer study their surroundings with eyes and ears on alert in case circumstances have changed.

But let's back up a little. Before you can even have beliefs, you need words to describe them, at least in most cases. And words are interesting things. After all, you cannot think intellectually without words. It's true. What was going through your mind when you were an infant and hadn't yet learned a language?

What if you were abused at a preverbal age? You wouldn't have any words to describe the event, would you? You would only have images and feelings without the intellectual ability to verbally process the information from that experience. How would that inability to use words to intellectualize affect the formation of your beliefs?

Now, let's take this conjectural scenario a step farther. If you were abused at a preverbal age, when you become an adult, you might have a very tough time putting your feelings about your early childhood into words. Instead, you may express yourself by acting out, such as throwing yourself onto the floor, having adult temper tantrums, scratching at your arms and legs, and periodically threatening to commit suicide. All this drama is to communicate how you feel when you remember the images of the abuse you experienced as a baby.

Sometimes, when I cannot find the words to express my feelings, I channel my emotions into some form of art, drawings, clay sculptures, or sketches. All these art forms and more can provide an avenue of expression that cannot always be obtained from verbal communication.

Although we all have suffered to some degree, the good news is we can change our beliefs from viewing ourselves as *victims* to viewing ourselves as *survivors*. Although we cannot change the past, we can learn from it and become wiser. In that way, we are reframing our beliefs about those past experiences.

If you believe you are a victim, it is time to update that belief. You are not that same person anymore, nor are you living in the past. Like a deer who doesn't assume everything is the same as before, you should realize that things have changed. It's time for a reality check. Since you lived through that experience, you are a *survivor*, not a victim. As of now, transform that old belief of being a victim and embrace your new belief as a survivor!

Do you feel the difference? Can you feel the energy shift? Being a victim is a helpless feeling; being a survivor is empowering! As an empowered individual, you are better positioned to understand and help others who have experienced similar abuse. You see, your new belief as a survivor has a purpose. That's turning a negative into a positive.

Likewise, just as there are no words at a preverbal age, there are also no words to describe particular emotions accurately. People who have deep feelings understand what this means. Human language is part of the physical world with physical references. Emotions are nonphysical, so words from the physical plane cannot precisely describe them. I, too, had emotional experiences that were indescribable. Somehow, those events gave birth to new beliefs within me—beliefs without words. Is this possible?

While we are on the topic of beliefs, labels are also words that create beliefs. These labels segregate us into roles, classes, and stereotypes. Unfortunately, after we form these preconceived beliefs, we tend to dismiss any evidence that doesn't fit our views. You can see how this type of thinking can quickly lead to prejudice. It's time to practice the wisdom of the deer and drop our assumptions about others and ourselves.

Today's Teaching from Mother Nature

Don't always believe your beliefs. Be like the deer and question your opinions—all of them! This activity takes courage because some of those beliefs formed the foundation upon which you built your life. Even so, be strong enough to question them. If your views still ring true to your authentic self, keep them. If not, drop them like a bad habit because that is what they are.

24
Access Your Instinctual Wisdom

There is a duality that exists in our lives. As humans, we are individuals, while at the same time made from other components and sources. Yes, we are separate entities, but also biological manifestations of our parents. And they are the manifestation of *their* parents, and so on. We can accept both aspects of our existence; we are separate yet empathically interconnected with everyone.

Since all people are part of humanity, it is not difficult to understand each other's basic needs. To do this, all you must do is understand yourself. Get in touch with your feelings. Be aware of your central biological and psychological needs and realize that everyone shares those basic needs and emotions across the globe.

Some believe that things are created from nothing; others believe that things can be 100 percent destroyed and cease to exist. But is this possible? An object cannot just come out of nothingness. This nothingness concept makes no sense because everything is something. It is not feasible for a thing to become a non-thing. Instead, things merely change from one form to another.

You, too, came from something. After you pass on, you'll become something else. In that way, you are eternal because you keep changing forms forever. Nothing is destroyed entirely. Everything that exists now is a continuation of what once existed, including you. Your body is composed of many elements, including oxygen, carbon, hydrogen, nitrogen, calcium, phosphorus, and so on. And the molecules within you are constantly changing. (Are you still paying attention? Did I lose you?)

Perhaps a visualization exercise will be helpful here. Picture a beautiful, lush forest. Animals lived and died in this place. Their decomposing bodies eventually become soil, providing nutrients for the surrounding plants. Now, picture those same plants, in turn, being eaten by the herbivores so they become part of the animals again. It's the circle of life.

Likewise, within your veins flows the blood of your ancestors. You are a continuation of their DNA. If you could trace your ancestral roots to the first few humans who walked on this planet, you would better understand how all people are related. Over the last two hundred thousand years, humans have migrated across the entire globe. Yet, we are all still human; we are one race. That's interconnectedness!

Since you have the inherited lineage of your ancestors within you, you can communicate with them intuitively. You can call on this *cellular wisdom* in times of need. The ancestors had life experiences that they passed down to you on a genetic level, which can help you in your current struggles. What, don't believe it? Well, how do you explain your instincts, then? Instincts are unlearned behaviors we are all born with. So, aren't instincts a form of genetic wisdom from our ancestors?

I remember when I needed to call upon the wisdom of my ancestors when I got lost while hiking in northern Minnesota near the Canadian border. I was staying in a cabin miles away from any house or town. I walked into the woods for what I thought would be a short hike. I was so mesmerized by the beautiful pine trees in the dense wetland forest that I wandered off the trail and got lost. I tried to find my way out by determining which way was north. Unfortunately, determining the four directions did me no good because I was so turned around that I had no clue which direction led back to the cabin.

I then had the bright idea of climbing one of the tallest pine trees to hopefully see the cabin or the dirt road.

I climbed up so high that I was hanging on to the very top part of the tree. The wind started to blow, and I began to sway back and forth with the breeze. Since the tree was already beginning to bend from my weight, I feared that the top part might break off under the stress of the additional wind. The last thing I needed was to fall and break my bones.

From a bird's-eye view, I quickly looked around to get my bearings. That is when the fear truly hit me because all I could see was a canopy of green treetops and nothing else—no cabin roof, no roads, and not even distant structures on the horizon. No landmarks were visible at all! I was so panicked that I just clung to the swaying treetop, not knowing what to do next.

For some reason, I started thinking about my ancestors; I don't know why. Maybe it was my instincts kicking in. I needed their wisdom to help me. I felt that a few of them certainly had had their adventures getting lost. But more to the point, I was only interested in the wisdom of those ancient relatives who had found their way back. No offense to the ancestorial spirits, but I didn't see the point in talking to the ones who'd wandered until they'd perished.

As soon as I made my mental request for help, I looked down and noticed a slight dip in the spacing of the brush beneath me. Was it the path? Yes! I immediately climbed down and followed the thin trail back to the cabin. I'd learned my lesson: I should never lose sight of my path in life, or I could become an ancestor myself sooner than expected.

Today's Teaching from Mother Nature

Today, take a stroll in nature. Make sure you do not get lost. Perhaps you would like to walk through a neighboring park, flower garden, or along a stream. Sit under a tree if you can. If you cannot leave home, sit near a window to view the trees or enjoy the sky.

Clear your mind of all your worries and concerns. Become aware of your breathing. Get in touch with your animal instincts by focusing on your physiology. Feel your heart beating in your chest. Deeply experience what it's like to be an organic being. Fill your mind with thoughts about your ancestors. Imagine how they looked when they were alive.

Let your mind go back farther now. Picture the smiling face of your great-great-great-grandfather and grandmother from several generations before you. How far back can you go? Allow your mind to wander freely. Follow the ancient footsteps back to the origins of humanity. Recognize the biological connection you have with all humans. This biology is your heritage; it is your interconnectedness to everyone who has ever lived! Embrace your global family and realize we are all one. With this new perspective, treat everyone as kindly as you would a loving family member.

25
A Drifting Breeze and a Flowing River

Most people want to become wiser. When it comes to the topic of wisdom, no one holds exclusive rights. Almost any experience in life teaches us practical lessons. Words need not be poetic and flowery to be full of insight. Common words are the easiest to understand and follow.

People who practice sage knowledge understand how to get along with others. They do not argue and squabble over differences of opinion. They know that trying to make someone else feel wrong is socially counterproductive and goes against common sense because it causes resentment.

Perhaps you can think of a few examples from your life when you were put down because you expressed your point of view. They may have insulted you, spoken to you condescendingly, and attempted to make you feel inferior just because you did not share their opinion. You know what that feels like—it hurts. The people who do such impolite things lack the wisdom of compassion. You don't want to be like them, do you?

If you publicly force people to admit they are wrong, you have only damaged their egos and polluted social relationships. Social pollution is not the wisdom of Mother Nature. The earth provides for you without demanding that you confess your faults. Nature has the power to show you a healthier way by example. You, too, can inspire people to live healthier by example rather than by trying to pressure and manipulate them into doing what you think is *right*.

I don't want to *impress*; I want to *inspire*. Yet, inspiring people does not mean trying to modify their personalities. Instead, changing and improving *my* attitude toward others is much wiser than trying to change *them*. Developing a more loving mindset for various personalities is one of the first steps in fostering inner wisdom. The richness of human diversity is one of the things that makes life more attractive.

Learn to let some things go. You do not need to respond to every comment. Instead of automatically reacting to something you disagree with, be emotionally detached.

Detachment does not mean you do not care. On the contrary, you may care a great deal. However, if you are emotionally married to your opinions, arguments inevitably ensue, and feelings can be easily hurt. Here, stubborn pride is the enemy. It is far better to let go of your need to be right. Instead, practice deep listening. There is wisdom in understanding the other person's perspective, even if you disagree.

Understanding others does not take a lot of exertion. Does it take much effort for the breeze to blow? Does the river put forth an enormous amount of energy to flow downstream? No. Nor does it require any incredible feat to relate to someone. All you need to do is ask yourself how you would feel if you were in their situation. A little empathy goes a long way. You develop more compassion when you start understanding what seeing the world through the other person's eyes is like.

Becoming a compassionate listener takes time, so be patient with yourself. Trust that positive things will happen in the long run. You do not need to rush your development. If you were gardening, would you become impatient with the new sprouts and plow them under because they were not growing fast enough for you? If you did, you would only succeed in uprooting them and destroying the very things you were trying so hard to nurture and grow. Take a deep breath and relax. Listening skills and empathy will ripen like fruit on the vine.

Let your life reflect the way of nature. Look to Mother Earth as a role model. Since the Giver of Life created nature, it stands to reason that nature's way is the Creator's way. So, step aside graciously and do not interfere with the course of Mother Nature. This noninterference requires you to let go of your stubborn will and be wise enough to ride the wave of loving energy that flows from all living things. Let the energy of the Creator flow naturally through you to all you meet.

Today's Teaching from Mother Nature

Remember that the breeze does not need to struggle; likewise, you can embrace the wisdom of nature effortlessly. Have a willingness to learn from the lessons Mother Earth has for you. You will be open to new ideas once you are humble enough to allow yourself to learn. Your fresh view of life will become as broad as the open sky.

As a specific activity, consider how a river flows without effort. Next, think of something you respect about your neighbor. It does not have to be a huge thing; it can be any characteristic you appreciate about that person. Then, give your neighbor a sincere compliment. If a conversation follows, practice the wisdom of listening with empathy. Try to see things from the other person's point of view regardless of how much your opinion differs.

26
Grandfather Sun Teaches by Example

Teaching is giving. A good example of perpetual giving is the sunshine that provides warmth and light to us without discriminating against anyone, like a nurturing grandfather. Grandfather Sun teaches us fairness because we all share solar benefits equally. We, too, can mirror our inner light just as the twinkling stars do when they reflect Grandfather Sun.

Some people may hold back on teaching others because they fear making mistakes. But everyone makes mistakes from time to time. That's how we learn and grow, so you don't have to fear messing up. Instead, view your blunders as learning opportunities to improve yourself. Then, like Grandfather Sun, you can openly teach these life lessons by being a good example without turning anyone away. When teaching, the trick is not to judge yourself too harshly for making errors. With this kind of freedom from self-judgment, you will be less likely to judge anyone else either.

Similarly, by having compassion for yourself, you will be able to show compassion to other individuals. Over time, you will discover you do not need to judge or reject anyone. With this frame of mind, you will be better able to teach people how to find relief from their turmoil by letting go of self-judgment. Moreover, you may enjoy doing this because acts of kindness give pleasure.

This lesson is best taught by role modeling, not sermon preaching. Usually, people are more concerned with being treated kindly than with a moral lecture. They don't want to be judged. So, instead of telling others what to do, *show* them what you do by demonstrating kindness. They will be watching you more than listening to you. Remember, your actions speak louder than the words you are saying. That is why it is usually best to lead by example. And besides, most of the time, the ones who talk the most tend to be the ones who understand the least. (Hmm, so why am I so wordy?)

I like to gently remind people who act as if they have all the answers that they are not keepers of the absolute truth. These know-it-alls stubbornly hold their ground. It's as if just considering the possibility that someone else's opinion has merit would shake the very foundation of their belief system. Ironically, it is their closed-mindedness that causes these smarty-pants elitists to stumble mentally. Do you know anyone like this? I bet you are picturing that person in your mind right now, aren't you?

However, we don't have to push our beliefs on anyone; that's my main point! A wise advisor doesn't force others to follow the advice. Instead, the sage mentor merely points to one of many possible paths we can choose. Regrettably, too many of us don't even look at the path ahead because we are too busy admiring the wise advisor. Isn't that the way it is? We get so caught up in the magnetism of our guides that we completely overlook the fact that they are trying to direct us to a better place.

We need to be well grounded before attempting to teach others. That is why we must let go of self-judgments when we make mistakes. We can learn from our blunders. Mother Nature teaches us life lessons, and then we teach others. So, be confident and secure in the wisdom of nature. Life experiences are the foundation of knowledge, building lessons upon lessons. When we feel connected to Mother Earth, we can demonstrate this understanding to others through how we live.

Part of the problem is people learned to view things in opposite extremes—all or none. They never knew (or forgot) that balance is the key to life. This balance is the basis of homeostasis. Nature strives for a perpetual homeostatic state, and so do humans. When people habitually see life through the narrow lens of right and wrong, they instantly become judgmental. They think that for some things to be good, others must be bad. When this type of irrational cognitive processing enters the mind, reasonableness instantly disappears as quickly as sight disappears after switching off the light in a windowless room.

When the opportunity does arise to teach others, you do not need to provide answers. Nor do you need to defend your beliefs. You can teach without speaking a word. After all, isn't that how Grandfather Sun teaches? You cannot force people to think your way. So, forget about imposing your will on others. Let them learn naturally. Just let your life lessons and inner light shine for all to see. Do not hide your sunshine. Be your natural self, and nature will lead you.

Please do not mistake this methodology as a nonaction approach to interpersonal relationships. It is not passivity. On the contrary, it is a call to action. Just emanate life energy while interacting with others. It is a form of action done effortlessly. Grandfather Sun knows how to do this. He remains stationary in the sky and may appear passive, yet much is being accomplished. The message is clear: Don't just talk, act!

People have been so disappointed by broken promises and misinformation that they are conditioned not to trust words. When it comes to incomprehensible topics, such as understanding the source of life energy, it seems that the human language cannot accurately describe this abstract realm. The more people try to sermonize on life's great mysteries, the less they truly understand. Inevitably, this leads to misinterpretations, misunderstandings, and arguments.

Ultimately, being your natural loving self without forcing things is most effective. Be a positive role model, then emotionally let go of trying to achieve results. If you are not emotionally married to a particular outcome, you are less likely to become defensive or try to prove yourself. And don't explain yourself, either. It is enough to let people see the effect of your actions, and they will learn from watching you.

Today's Teaching from Mother Nature

Teach your life lessons without pushing so much. Instead of forcing an issue, be like Grandfather Sun and let positive energy radiate naturally from you. Do you have enough self-discipline to teach others without imposing your will? As you go about your day, try demonstrating knowledge without words. Let go of your desire to control the people and events around you. Allow nature to follow its course without your interference. As with Grandfather Sun, you teach by example when you share the warmth in your heart.

27
Lightning Knows the Source of Life

Anything alive has life energy. However, the basis of that energy is not so clear. What is it? Where is it located? How can we measure it? Is it physical or metaphysical—or both? Is a Higher Power or Source the cause? I don't have the answers because I don't think humans can understand the Source of life entirely. Therefore, be wary of the self-admiring guru who claims to have all the answers. At first blush, these charlatans can appear attractive because they provide easy answers to life's most difficult questions. But the Source rarely gives easy answers.

The Source of life is too vast to simplify into human words. We can feel the life energy inside us, yet we cannot describe what initially sparked that energy. Speaking of sparks, a campfire crackles and pops with energy, but do we understand where that energy originated? Lightning flashes, but is there anything more to it than just the scientific explanation? Fireflies twinkle with a pulsating glow, but what is beyond the exothermic chemical reactions? From lightning bolts to lightning bugs, we see and feel the life energy yet cannot define the Source in words. Vocabulary has its limits.

Ironically, the more we try to explain the unexplainable, the more confused we get. Ancient wisdom teaches that the more we learn about the Source, the more there is to know. The challenge is to stay consciously connected to the Source. One suggestion for doing this is to be aware that you already possess life energy. Therefore, you have a connection to the essence of that energy. If you didn't, you wouldn't be alive! Once you acknowledge this connection, you can let the energy from the Source flow through you and out to others.

One of the most frequently asked questions on this topic is how you let this energy flow from yourself to other people. Let's say, for example, you were hosting a dinner party at your home. Let's also assume you care about your guests and their feelings; you want them to have a relaxing and enjoyable time. Your concern for them is a form of love. When you show this love for other people, life energy from the Source automatically wells up within you. It radiates from you like the glow parents get when they hold their newborn child. This energy affects everything you say and do.

In the dinner party example, you can show this positive energy with a bright smile as you greet your arriving guests, which makes them feel comfortable and right at home. Eventually, they take their seats at the table, and your smile becomes infectious. Soon, all your guests will smile and laugh as they enjoy each other's company.

The life energy from the Source continues to flow through you as you serve them food, fill their glasses, and make sure they have everything they need for a satisfying meal. Your guests can sense you care about them and can feel the positive life energy in you. This compassion is something you cannot fake. If you try to pretend, you end up looking insincere.

In restaurants, perhaps you have experienced being waited on by overworked and frustrated servers. Despite the simulated smiles on their faces, you could tell they were feeling run down. It is probably more accurate to say that those servers resented having to work when they were feeling so tired. You could see it in their eyes. If the servers truly had the energy of life flowing through them, they might have appreciated the opportunity to bring joy to other people. From that perspective, servitude is a gift.

Being attentive is also a gift you can share with those around you. This is yet another way to let the Source flow through you. When you pay attention and listen to someone, you communicate to them that they are important. They can sense you care about them without saying so because listening is loving.

The next time your coworkers, friends, neighbors, children, or romantic partner approaches you with something on their minds, let them know how much you care about them by turning off the TV, putting down the phone, and giving them your full attention. Turn your back to the computer screen and focus instead on the living person right before you. This is called being in the present moment, and it is a beautiful thing.

There are so many opportunities to share life energy with people. This type of sharing does not mean you need to deplete your physical energy supply. Instead, you can mentally tap into the Source. Allow that positive energy to pass through you and enrich the lives of everyone you meet. That way, you do not get burned out because you are not draining your internal resources. Alternatively, you rely on an external resource to provide loving energy.

Today's Teaching from Mother Nature

Lightning has energy and a connection to the Source of life, and so do you. Before you go to bed tonight, please recognize the connection you already have with the Source. Once you acknowledge this connection, open those valves of loving energy and let the Source flow out to all the people in your life.

28
That Mysterious Being Within Us

Whenever I receive recognition for some accomplishment, I mention that the proper credit goes to the Mysterious Being within me. What do I mean by Mysterious Being? Well, let me put it this way—it is the life energy that sees through my eyes. Let me ask you a few thought-provoking questions. Who do you become when you fall asleep each night? What Mysterious Being keeps your heart beating? What exactly is life?

If you think you can reason your way to understanding this Mysterious Being, you will find that your thoughts tumble around in your head like fall leaves blowing across the ground. It cannot be truly understood directly, only peripherally. It's like trying to see a faint star in the night sky. You see it out of the corner of your eye, but when you look directly at it, it vanishes. However, if you use your peripheral vision and look to one side of that dim star, it becomes visible again.

Comparably, if you try to understand the Mysterious Being by directly thinking about it, it eludes you. When you chase after it, you chase it away. Alternatively, by viewing the Mysterious Being peripherally, you can see a bit more of it. It's as if you sense it from the edge of your subconscious awareness. This does not imply in any way that you can completely understand it. Claiming a complete understanding of such an unknowable mystery would be conceited and a false impression.

Let's play with this idea for a minute. Do you know some people who claim to understand the Mysterious Being fully? Perhaps they think their beliefs are the *only* correct thoughts and everyone else is wrong. Have you noticed they use an authoritarian tone when speaking about their beliefs? As if they were dictatorially giving marching orders, they tend to tell other people how to live because they think they know what is best for everyone.

The problem with this grandiose thinking is that it's incredibly self-congratulatory because they set themselves above everyone else. Conversely, it also creates a feeling of separation from those who disagree. The more they put themselves on a pedestal, the more they distance themselves from their fellow human beings. This is the opposite of interconnectedness.

When they make a habit of separating themselves from others, they end up feeling lonelier, which can eventually lead to some form of depression. They may be unable to control these feelings, so let's not blame them for their sadness. It also needs to be stated that there are many forms and many causes of depression. This hypothetical example is not meant to be a complete list.

Perhaps you also know some other extremists who have moments of excessive elation when they convince themselves they know the will of the Mysterious Being. Of course, these emotional highs inevitably have bouts of equally deep lows where they feel socially disconnected and alone. They go back and forth between the highs and lows. Their emotional volatility can ruin marriages and can put a strain on any relationship. These mood swings are not their fault; ultimately, they need our understanding and compassion. Hopefully, they will seek a doctor's care.

You may have noticed that when you've expressed your concern, they've refused to believe there was a problem. They typically deny anything that contradicts their opinions. Can you see how their dogmatic attitude perpetuates separation, not interconnectedness? Before you can even finish your sentence, they dismiss any contrary evidence as deception or false information. Is this a pretty good description of some stubborn people you know? This is why it is so important to have an open mind and acknowledge that you do not fully understand the Mysterious Being.

Today's Teaching from Mother Nature

Close your eyes and sit in silence for fifteen minutes. Do not try to hang on to any thoughts. Let your feelings come and go. Visualize your thoughts slowly tumbling down like dried leaves falling off a tree in autumn and settling on the ground.

In the silence, reach out with your senses and feel the presence of the Mysterious Being—that life energy within you. Feel your heart beating and recognize that energy is pure love. Now, feel the interconnectedness you share with the life energy of every being on the planet. Feel what that is like for you. Then open your eyes and start living life with the understanding you are one with all living things. The Mysterious Being within you connects with the Mysterious Being in all others. After all, life energy is life energy in any form.

29
Wisdom from Your Inner Animal

It dawned on me one day that many of the struggles I go through in life are a direct result of my acting counter to my nature. For instance, I was unhappy and stressed when I tried to be what other people wanted me to be. On the other hand, when I did what I felt was natural for me, I was more joyful and emotionally free. Consequently, I learned to pay close attention to my instinctual feelings to keep me on my true path.

Have we become desensitized to our instincts? It's as if our whole society has slipped into a state of numbness. The comforts, luxuries, and conveniences of modern life dull our senses. Whatever happened to stepping outside the comfort zone? To truly benefit from the wisdom of nature, you need to engage with it. Engagement means taking an active role. Being engaged is not the same as being connected. The fact is, you are already connected to nature and always have been. Humanity is part of nature, not separate from it. However, if you are unaware of your connection, you will not recognize it.

Furthermore, you cannot learn the teachings of nature unless you interact with it. You can immerse yourself in the environment by walking and noticing all the living things around you, from the beings that crawl on the ground to the beings that fly in the sky. Animals, including humans, adapt to the ever-changing environment. The key to adaptation is to keep instincts sharp.

So, how sharp are *your* instincts? How well do you adapt? When smaller birds pester an eagle, the eagle flies to a higher altitude where the little hecklers cannot go. Can you rise above your problems like the eagle who sees the big picture? Are you quick, like the hummingbird who dashes from blossom to blossom, finding opportunities everywhere? Do you have the stamina of the bear who endures the long winters? Are you as graceful as a cat that moves through the day so smoothly it resembles liquid motion?

It's imperative to keep in touch with your inner animal. Unlike what you see in popular movies, you do not need to fight to be the king of the jungle. After all, a lion doesn't need to rule the environment to thrive in it. Likewise, you do not have to strive to be the alpha beast by dominating others. Instead, you can communicate with your animal instincts and listen to that wisdom and guidance.

We need to live simpler lives. Animals know how to do this. They do not complicate their lives with unnecessary busyness and hoarding possessions. However, humans so often do. Why? Do all these needless activities and possessions make our lives better or worse? Buying that little shiny something that catches our eye in a store may feel good, and we convince ourselves we can't live without it. But we soon discover those sparkling objects lose their appeal after a time, and then we are out shopping again for the next piece of glitter.

Remember that the less you have, the less you can lose. You cannot strengthen your inner animal by accumulating possessions. Surrounding yourself with needless objects weakens your ability to focus on your instincts because all that clutter distracts you. Instead of cooperating with the natural order of things, advertisers act like we can live forever if we use their anti-wrinkle cream, drink their expensive water in fancy designer bottles, and get a good facelift.

Society seems to be obsessed with staying eternally young. Do you think nature designed humans to stay young forever? Physical immortality is a separation from the natural world. Since you cannot truly separate yourself from nature, you might as well accept the fact you will eventually die. True, all animals have an instinct to survive, including you. Therefore, do your best to survive, live as healthily as possible, and not worry about things beyond your control, like death from natural causes.

Today's Teaching from Mother Nature

Engage with nature. Be mindful of your instincts and follow the wisdom of your inner animal. This may give you a more profound sense of peace. When you experience this new inner peace, your true nature can soar higher than an eagle and accomplish more than you thought possible. Just don't expect applause. After all, most people are so wrapped up in their concerns that they don't even notice the majestic eagles in the sky. So, don't be surprised if they don't see *your* accomplishments, either.

30
Finding Pure Love in the Abyss

Recently, I contemplated the topic of light. I had many questions. I wondered about the different energies between light and darkness. Furthermore, I remembered that I'd experienced positive energy in the darkness. My awareness was raised by the thought that there is also a type of light found in the darkness—black light. White light is not better than black light. They balance each other.

No light can exist without darkness because light needs something to contrast. Everything in the universe is connected. Nothing can exist in complete isolation by itself. Therefore, light can only exist in relationship with complementary darkness. What's significant to understand is that there is loving energy in all forms of light, including black light.

Many people have a negative, even fearful, interpretation of darkness. They talk about moving out of the darkness and into the light. Or they say something along the lines of being delivered from the darkness. They seem to forget that Mother Nature is life energy, and life energy is everywhere, including in the loving darkness of the abyss. There is no rational need to be afraid of the darkness. After all, we enter the darkness every time we close our eyes and fall asleep. And keep in mind that we all began life in the darkness when we were conceived. We weren't afraid of the dark when we were in the womb. Besides, the Creator gave birth not only to light but also to darkness. So, it can't be all bad, right? If darkness is so terrible, then why did the Creator create it?

Look at it this way: Suppose a mental garden exists in our minds. Some areas in that garden are full of bright light where wonderful emotional things grow, such as compassion and understanding. We give some of these things away to others when we do acts of kindness. Our cerebral garden also blooms in positive actions, usually as verbal support—loving words, compliments, and encouragement.

And then, a dimly lit area in this mysterious garden with a black light throws shadows. However, that dark area is not a hole; holes have bottoms. This dark patch has no bottom because it is a tunnel, a time tunnel that leads to faraway places from our past. Looking into the tunnel is like looking into the abyss. I know we are getting deeply philosophical here. (Just hang on and enjoy the ride.)

Many years ago, I was invited to do a mental imagery exercise for personal development. It involved closing my eyes and imagining I was peering into the dark abyss. Well, I'm not one to only sneak a peek, so I envisioned myself diving into the abyss headfirst as if it were a deep, dark pool, and I was swimming to the bottom. I figured, hey! In for a penny, in for a pound, right?

That is when I discovered the abyss has no bottom; instead, it is a dark tunnel of black light with positive energy. I swam through this tunnel and came out on the other side into the white light. It made me think of being in the womb and being born. I concluded from this visualization that since I came from the womb's darkness and was born into the light, I am a being of both black and white light—yin and yang. Does this make sense, or have I lost you off the deep end of the dark pool?

Today's Teaching from Mother Nature

Instead of trying to fix your problems by digging your way out of a hole, imagine that the hole is a tunnel you need to work through to come out victorious on the other side. Don't be afraid to dive into the emotional abyss in your mind. Swim down deep and see what's there. You may discover, as I did, that it's a tunnel. Yes, it's a dark tunnel, but as stated earlier, life energy is everywhere, and the black light in the abyss is full of loving energy. This understanding can lead to a more profound sense of emotional awareness.

Tonight, as you are lying in bed drifting off to sleep, close your eyes and enter the darkness as you usually do. Picture yourself going into this loving space of black light. Imagine you are back in the womb, warm and safe. Let yourself experience pure loving energy and be open to whatever lessons you may learn from this experience. Be sure to journal on it.

31

Do Not Force the Flower to Open

I don't know about you, but I should develop more patience. That's just one of many attitude adjustments I am making. My impatience was illustrated quite clearly one spring day when I was anxiously waiting for an exceptional flower to bloom in my garden. It already had a bud that was just on the verge of opening. I waited until the next day, but the bud had not fully opened. It was only half open. So, why the delay?

Oh, I suppose I could have let it go another day, but it was my favorite flower, and I couldn't wait! After all, I have already waited through the entire winter to see this unique flower bloom. How can I be expected to sit by while Mother

Nature takes Her sweet time? You can probably guess where this is going, huh? Yep, that's right; I tried to force the flower petals to open.

As a warm breeze blew over the garden, I gently stuck my intrusive fingers into the bud and slowly peeled back some of the outside petals. Yes, many of them got torn. I could see the petals folding around each other like a tangled bunch of wet socks twisted at the bottom of my washing machine.

The flower was not ready to open, but my impatience would not allow me to delay my gratification one second longer! As a result of my impulsiveness, I had a shredded flower hanging from the stem, and it looked like it had gone through a hurricane. That's when I realized I needed to improve my impatient attitude.

So, what lesson did I glean from this experience? Well, many things come to mind, not the least of which is to be more accepting of nature's way. Incidentally, this attitudinal adjustment applies to my interactions with humans as well. There are numerous examples in my past where I became impatient with people who did not change their behavior fast enough to meet my expectations.

Perhaps there is a lesson we can all learn from this. We need to accept people's personalities the way they are without trying to change them. The exception, of course, is if someone's behavior is violent, verbally abusive, or otherwise criminal. In brief, we need to practice more compassion and less criticism.

Accepting people without trying to change them was particularly challenging for me since I worked for many years as a counselor. People would come to me seeking advice because they wanted to improve their lives. That was why they'd scheduled the appointment in the first place. How could I not try to change them? Well, I eventually learned that they needed to change themselves. I could only be a guide on the side.

As you might imagine, it is more than just a little ironic that I am now writing about how to help you improve yourself while at the same time embracing the belief that I should accept you the way you are. The fact that I am encouraging you to stop trying to change others means I'm trying to change you.

Allow me to clarify. (Well, it's not so much a clarification as a justification.) With my new attitude, I am simply putting positive messages out there for anyone who wants them. Then, I let go of any emotional attachments to the outcome. If people accept my messages, that's fine. If they don't, that's fine, too. That way, I have no emotional investment in changing people. Instead, I am just serving an intellectual buffet of friendly suggestions for anyone who wishes to dine.

Not only is it valuable to be patient with other people, but it is also imperative to be patient with yourself. Any new mindset, attitude, or change of perspective takes time to develop into long-standing cognitive patterns. After all, a river needs time to carve a gorge. Likewise, your new thoughts need time to establish deeply entrenched neuropathways in your brain.

Today's Teaching from Mother Nature

If you choose, you can make some changes in your life. Take an honest look at your attitude. Does it need some fine-tuning? Are you as patient as you would like to be? Can you accept people for who they are, provided they do not cause harm?

Now is the time to examine your perspective of the world. It's a type of soul-searching, if you will. What thoughts, beliefs, outlooks, mindsets, and opinions do you want to keep, and which do you want to eliminate? It's your choice. This inner work comes from *you*, not others imposing *their* will on you.

If you have a few characteristics you want to change, write them down. It helps to make a written list to look at occasionally. Seeing this list will remind you of your new goals, so place the list where you will see it often.

I found that changing my attitude also changed my worldview. I am more patient now and have fewer unreasonable expectations of others. Consequently, I feel more at peace with myself. I wish the same for you.

32
Extinguish the Fires of Resentment

Hostility spreads like wildfire. A tiny spark of aggression can sweep through an entire group quickly. Maybe you have experienced what it is like to walk into a room just after a heated argument. Even though the yelling ended minutes ago, you can still sense the hostility and tension in the air. Anger sweeps through the room like an inferno and affects everyone's mood. Those fiery emotions can scorch your mood for the rest of the day.

In a way, strong emotions have a certain stickiness about them. This emotional stickiness is like walking through the tall grass where wood ticks are known to congregate. Some ticks will eventually latch on to you, and you will carry them around. If you are not highly vigilant, you could inadvertently take those ticks home, where they could harm your family. This analogy is one of many ways to illustrate how strong, negative emotions can stay with you and affect those around you.

Here's a hypothetical example to illustrate this point: Imagine you had a conversation with a woman who spent her whole life being angry and resentful. While talking to her, she went on and on about how she felt abandoned by her ex-spouse. Imagine hearing her raspy voice spitting out searing words as she proclaimed that she would never forgive her ex-husband.

Although their marriage ended some twenty years ago, she thought he was to blame for all her current problems. She believed it was because of him that she never found a stable romantic relationship after the divorce, was unable to hold down a job longer than a couple of months, was unhappy with her life, and had poor mental health. For the sake of simplicity, we will assume that her mental health issues were a preexisting condition before the marriage.

So, who was she hurting? Is any of her bitterness improving her life? Is her resentment truly punishing her ex-husband? Of course not. He probably moved on with his life years ago and now considers his former marriage part of the distant past. We can only wish she would do the same.

But nay. Let's pretend that this jilted ex-spouse is now taking things a step farther by talking to you about getting her revenge on him someday. She has it all figured out. She fanaticizes about inadvertently running into him at a store and screaming in his face, telling him how much she hates him for what he did to her. She wants to let him have it! However, what she fails to consider as she attempts to metamorphose herself into a marriage avenger superhero is the enormous emotional cost to herself. By obsessing over past hurts, she is sacrificing the joys of the present moment.

Forgiveness is needed here, not revenge. Remember, forgiveness does not excuse the dysfunctional behavior of the offender. Revenge is analogous to being able only to smell something sweet and delectable but not being able to eat it. Sadly, merely smelling something delicious doesn't truly satisfy the appetite. I wish it did. (Sigh.)

If you prefer a different metaphor, try this one: Resentment is like walking through poison ivy; you leave the plant behind, but you carry the itchy oil with you. Whatever way you look at it, these negative emotions are highly destructive and can deleteriously affect you and those closest to you.

There are many ways to curb anger before it reaches resentment. One of my favorite cognitive techniques is to let go of my unrealistic expectations. Sometimes, I think of people as seeds in my vegetable garden. Some seeds will sprout and be productive, while others will not meet my expectations. It does me no good to get angry at a vegetable just because its shape and size do not meet my standards. Similarly, it does no good for me to get angry with people just because they believe differently.

The ability to let go of unrealistic expectations has never been more important than in an intimate relationship. A highly destructive element in any relationship is when one person tries to force the other to change. Even if the individual in question needs help badly, as with chemical dependency issues, it will not be beneficial to try to push that person to change. And don't even think about using manipulation and guilt tactics because they do not work long term. Unless the person is ready to change and truly wants it, the recovery will not last.

So many couples fight over every little thing. What they don't do is work as a team on common goals. Traffic moves smoothly down the freeway when each car goes in the same direction in their respective lanes. So, too, it is with intimate relationships. So, team up!

A surefire way for you to feel happier is to help someone else feel happier. A simple way to do this daily is to give more compliments. Spoiler alert: Don't be surprised if the people you compliment do not thank you. Not everyone is going to be grateful. Realizing and accepting this can help you let go of the expectation for reciprocation. That way, you won't feel disappointed if they do not respond.

It's hard to see the positive qualities in others when you are feeling angry. What helps is first to let the bitterness settle down like murky water. This reminds me of one of my favorite hobbies—looking for agates in the shallow water along the shoreline of Lake Superior. If my feet stir up the water too much, I can't see the prized stones like undiscovered treasures at the bottom.

How often do you unnecessarily stir up the waters of relationships with negative emotions like resentment and bitterness? When your mind is not otherwise preoccupied with the muddy thoughts of past hurts, you will find the cognitive clarity to see more positive things. With this new perspective, you will recognize more of the beauty all around you.

Today's Teaching from Mother Nature

We've covered quite a bit here, including wildfires of bitterness, wood ticks of resentment, and muddy waters of past hurts. Let me fold it all together for you; it all comes down to forgiveness. That is the common theme. Once you let go of aggression and bitterness, you can experience the positive energy of forgiving others. Just as the goodness of Mother Earth is everywhere, you, too, can bring your best to everything you do. Contemplate how your life energy is the same life force in all people. Respect and honor that positive energy.

33
Chasing the Scared Cat of Happiness

Okay, here's the thing—happiness is like trying to run after a frightened house cat. The more you chase it, the more it runs away. Not until you stop, sit down, and be still will the cat of happiness come to you in its own good time. Trying to catch happiness reminds me of when I was a small child and tried to catch my shadow; I could never hold on to it.

When you overanalyze your happiness, it slips away. In other words, when you ask yourself if you are happy, you stop feeling happy because you are scrutinizing it. So, don't overthink your contentment. It's a concept as old as philosophy itself. When people ask me if I am happy, I usually say that I'm too busy being joyful to worry about whether I am happy.

The problem with asking yourself if you are happy is that it takes your awareness of what is going on around you at that moment and draws attention to idealistic expectations. The implied expectancy is that you *should* be happy. And once you start focusing on the shoulds in life, inevitably, feelings of guilt follow for not living up to those impractical standards. The message that seems to come from society is that you should always be content; if you are not, something is wrong with you. You miss the joy of fully appreciating the present by focusing on the shoulds.

If I break it down to the basics, I think there are two types of happiness—short term and long term. Both types are emotionally based. I believe short-term happiness stems from the emotions of excitement and stimulation, and long-term happiness grows from the feelings of inner peace and life satisfaction.

For example, you can buy a new gold watch that excites you. And, yes, that type of excitement is a form of happiness, but that is not the only type of pleasure because the excitement of a purchase eventually wears off. You may recall the excitement when you graduated from school. However, years later, when you look at that diploma, do you still feel the same excitement and start jumping for joy? Of course not. The short-term happiness wore off.

Long-term happiness, on the other hand, is based on inner peace. That type of happiness is an issue of personal integrity. You don't get integrity shopping in a store or from the excitement you feel when your favorite sports team wins. Instead, long-term happiness comes from living by your values, not the values others try to place on you. Typically, this type of happiness develops with time, age, and maturity as you establish more confidence. Then, that long-term contentment can bring your life a sense of purpose.

A negative mindset can exacerbate unhappiness. Not all unhappiness can be attributed to attitude, but much of it can be. If people are unhappy and suffering because they do not believe they have enough material possessions, then they should consider all the good things in their lives and blessings. People can learn to be satisfied with what they already have. It may not be all they want, but it is usually enough.

In a capitalistic society emphasizing materialism, we are programmed to be perpetually unsatisfied. We are constantly being told to buy more. Advertisements are everywhere we look, bombarding us with the message that we are not complete unless we purchase their products. Advertisements are constantly making us feel as though we lack something. After years of this conditioning, we think that enough is never enough. We continually feel we need more stuff to be happy, at least for the short term.

This endless craving for ever greater consumption also ties in with the issue of, dare I say it, addiction! With any addiction, people want more, more, more. They are pursuing short-term happiness because if that happiness were long term, they wouldn't continually need more. Whether they are chronically hitting the slot machines, excessively shopping, or compulsively playing video games, it appears that people suffering from addiction soon become immune to the ephemeral excitement of short-term happiness. Therefore, they constantly need additional thrills to give them another temporary happiness fix.

I think addictive activities initially provide brief satisfaction but eventually lead to misery. They may start engaging in addictive behavior to feel good, but once hooked, they are compelled to keep going to stop feeling bad. That's the trap!

Today's Teaching from Mother Nature

Don't run around franticly chasing that proverbial cat of happiness because it will bolt and hide from you. Instead, to achieve greater joy in the long term, first try letting go of your ego-fueled desires. You know the ones. They include insisting on having things your way, imposing your will on those around you, criticizing people, and defending your opinion in an argument because you are so sure you are right.

The next step to longer-lasting happiness is to limit those incessant wants, those never-ending desires for more, more, more! You have basic needs, of course, which are requirements for survival; that's a given. But there is a difference between needs and wants. The constant wants will keep you dissatisfied, feeling incomplete, restless, and unhappy. Be satisfied with what you have. Put another way, if you want your cup to overflow, get a smaller cup.

34

A Bear Taught Me About My Instincts

Animals are not the only ones with instincts. We humans also have instincts. These qualities are a wonderful thing. However, we can get into trouble when we ignore our instincts. That is why we ought to be mindful and attentive to our surroundings.

Incidentally, just because I have animal instincts, that doesn't mean I always use them. Case in point: I encountered a sow bear at close range because I did not listen to my instincts. Instead of fleeing, I tried to analyze the situation logically. How foolish of me?

Here's what happened. I was jogging with my dog down a country road at night when I heard something scurry off through the bushes and up a nearby tree. When I jog at night, I carry a flashlight, so I shined the light into the upper branches and saw glowing eyes looking down at me. I was trying to analyze what kind of animal it was. I thought it could be a raccoon or a bear cub; both are about the same size.

Then I heard a strange sound. It sounded like branches breaking. Snap, snap, snap. Curious to find out what that sound was, I took a few more steps into the woods. That is when the sound turned into a deep, growling snort. I didn't find out until later, but that commotion I heard in the bushes was the mother bear just a few feet away from where I was standing. She was snapping her jaws angrily and huffing, which reminded me of a snorting bull. My dog was more intelligent than me; she didn't need to analyze the situation to determine danger nearby. She stayed back on the gravel road, barking.

Meanwhile, back in the woods, I stupidly stood there thinking analytically. Instead of moving back, I was trying to figure out if that was a bear in the brush making those noises. The problem was that I could not see clearly; I just heard the noises. Finally, my instincts communicated the message to me: I was in danger! I felt the hair on my neck stand up, and I got the hell out of there!

Later, I read more about the behavior of bears. Based on that information, I concluded that the smaller animal in the tree was a bear cub. The much larger animal in the bushes was the mother bear. I shudder when I read that mother bears usually do not back down when defending their young.

When a cub feels threatened, it usually makes a bawling distress sound, which causes the sow bear to come to the cub's defense. If that baby bear had started crying when I was in the woods that night, I hate to think what could have happened to me. I should've responded to my instincts quicker.

For most of us, the danger is not from a wild animal but rather from a hostile work environment. Imagine a hypothetical work situation where your coworkers and you share a small office. What if they made up their minds that they don't like you? For whatever reason, they seem to take great pleasure in treating you coldly. They won't speak to you and only talk to each other. In other words, they cut you out of their conversations and want you to know it. And, what if you did your best to be kind and courteous to them by wishing them a good morning at the beginning of each workday, but they never replied—not even once!

Eventually, you will realize you cannot change them to suit your needs or force them to like you. So, what if you sidestepped the battle instead of fighting them and resisting the situation? What might be the results if you elected to feel sorry for them because they seem so unhappy?

I understand this level of compassion is not easy. However, you could choose not to think with your animal instincts but alternatively use your higher self and engage your brain in moral reasoning. You could make up your mind to be a compassionate person, not only to them but to everyone. It is a conscious decision to have a positive attitude no matter the situation.

This visualization technique might help: Picture yourself sitting at your desk. Now imagine a small glass heart filled with glowing white light. Then, imagine using your foot to slide that radiant heart across the floor to the people around you. In this way, you are sending them pure light and compassion.

So, what effect could this mental technique have on your coworkers? Well, you probably will not see any significant change in their behavior. But here's the thing—it changes *your* mood for the better, which makes it all worthwhile. So, even if they do not feel that positive energy you send them, *you* feel it, which can give you inner tranquility. This whole experience of working with other people can teach you how to be more compassionate. That's the benefit.

Today's Teaching from Mother Nature

Although it is unlikely that you will ever face an angry mama bear, be mindful of your animal instincts and analytical reasoning. Raise your awareness and realize you are already using both qualities every day. Act mindfully, not mindlessly. Instead of impulsively reacting to a situation, thoughtfully decide what you want to do. Then, act decisively. Don't wait for the proverbial bear to make the first move.

35

Your Energy Affects Other People

Your energy is your essence. Every time you speak, you are adding energy to the world. Is it positive or negative energy? Well, that is up to you. If you want to become more loving, you need to speak lovingly. That starts with thinking loving thoughts.

Okay, let's get practical. How exactly do you train your mind to think more positive thoughts? Well, it all starts with what you focus on in life. We are talking about your perception here. If you perceive humanity as one big family, with everyone being your brothers and sisters, then you will be more likely to speak kindly to them and less likely to harm them intentionally.

Before you can *perceive* something, you need to *conceive* it first. If you cannot conceive the notion of kindness in the world, you will not be able to perceive the kindness around you. If you cannot imagine having compassion for your fellow human beings, it is doubtful you will speak compassionately to them.

We receive so many negative messages and images from the news media daily that it can affect how we perceive things. After a while, the world can look hostile and dangerous. We react to this threat by seeking safety in what is familiar to us. Typically, that means sticking with old habits, not taking risks, avoiding strangers, and being guarded against anyone different from us. Unfortunately, this can sow the seeds of prejudice.

However, there is another way of thinking and perceiving the world. You can train yourself to think more positively and minimize the pessimistic view. This will improve your emotional energy and brighten your outlook. You can look for the good in others. Oh, yes, it's there! It may take a while to see it in certain people, but you will eventually find it; keep looking.

Here's a practical example of how a negative thought pattern can be turned around: As you sit at home in your living room watching TV, notice how your mind responds to the violence you see on the screen. This response is most likely the result of the media's conditioning of the public.

Once you are aware of this negative influence, you are in a place where you can do something positive about it and let your bright personality shine.

So, what can you do? One way to improve your thoughts is to ask yourself more constructive questions. When you see these violent images in a movie, ask yourself how to improve things. Perhaps that could mean turning the channel to watch a comedy show. Better yet, turn the TV off and spend more time with your loved ones.

It can benefit you greatly to realize how much your mind plays an active part in your happiness. Your thoughts directly affect your perception. And when you have more positive energy, that will eventually impact the quality of your life. If you want to see a dramatic improvement in your life, keep asking how to improve things. Ask yourself that question all day long, day after day. When you do, you will not only think differently, but you will also feel different. And those closest to you will notice the improvement in your character.

Okay, now that we have covered the area of thoughts, let's dive right into the area of behaviors. If you are serious about becoming a more loving person and having a more significant favorable influence on the world, then action is required. You cannot just sit there thinking happy thoughts while the proverbial house burns down around you. It is time to put what you learned into practice.

Of course, we are starting with the premise that you have already accomplished the previously stated task of *conceiving* loving thoughts and *perceiving* everyone as your sibling. The next step is to act in the other person's best interest. This step does not mean you neglect your needs, nor does it mean you allow someone to take advantage of you. It simply means being concerned about the well-being of the other person.

What could you do differently the next time you are in a store waiting in the checkout line and notice that the person just behind you has only a few items? This scenario is one of those opportunities to show kindness. You could let that other shopper go ahead of you. Whether your kindness is accepted or rejected, you have turned positive thoughts into positive actions.

You do not need to force it. Once you have positive thoughts, you need only let your essence glow as that energy flows from you. Compassion is not a sales pitch you push on others. Just let the love in your heart shine through naturally as if it were water seeking the lowest and most humble place.

In time, you will see more and more chances to show kindness. These opportunities are everywhere, including your home, school, shops, public places, and job. The more you recognize them, the more you will behave optimistically. And the more you let your true self shine and spread positive energy, the more it will come back to you because love loves to love more love. It is the law of attraction.

Today's Teaching from Mother Nature

Radiate loving energy to the world. Pause before you speak or act. Decide to put more positive energy into society rather than negative. Hold thoughts of love in your mind by thinking about what would be best for others. Then, let the kind words naturally flow from you. And if you see an opportunity to show compassion, by all means, do it!

36
Be the Porcupine and Use Your Quills

There are times when we overthink. It's as though all our worrisome thoughts are squawking birds fluttering about in our heads and driving us batty. We lose our inner peace and tranquility if we overanalyze everything and agonize about what could go wrong. Unfortunately, when we spend too much time scrutinizing a problem, we usually get mentally stuck and do not take decisive action. We need to start taking steps to solve the problem. Put candidly, we need to get off the couch and do something!

There are moments when we are so afraid to make a mistake that we don't act. In the long run, what difference does it make if we make a few mistakes along the way? We can recognize those mistakes early and correct them as we go. The point is to get going.

Sometimes, we hold off acting simply because we want to make someone else happy. Perhaps we are worried that our decision will displease those around us. However, life is not a popularity contest. If we genuinely believe a course of action is best, we can proceed with our plans, provided they don't hurt anyone. We do not need to let other people's opinions sway us from following our principles. To live life according to the likes and dislikes of others is ludicrous.

It is a trap to desperately seek someone's approval because your behavior becomes so limited. Fear of rejection can paralyze you and stop you from following your true path and natural calling. If you are worried about whether people are going to agree with your actions, you emotionally imprison yourself. In such a case, it's as though the chains of public approval bind your behavior.

These chains will keep you from living freely and acting on your life goals. This can become a vicious circle because when your mind is caught up in seeking approval, you subconsciously scrutinize everything you do to the point that nothing gets done. You may start a project, but you don't finish it.

If you step back from the tendency to overthink things, you realize that you do not need to view life so seriously.

Draw a slow, deep breath and ease up. You do not need to measure up to or contend with anyone. You will find a more profound sense of self-respect and serenity when you stop competing with the world to be the top dog. Likewise, when others see your calmness and sense your inner peace, they might respect you more.

Let's look at a fictional example: Picture a single woman (let's call her Rachel) who wants to make everyone happy. She is a people pleaser. At work, she lets her bullying boss walk all over her. He dumps his work responsibilities off on her, and she lets him without protesting. Now, some would say Rachel is just a good employee. However, let's also imagine that she feels exploited by her boss. He never even thanks her.

Rachel goes home after work and dwells on what happened that day. She thinks about how her boss mistreats her, and she becomes madder and madder. She stews about this issue for hours, sometimes losing sleep over it. Not once does she act on her convictions. Not once does she talk to her boss about her feelings. Not once does she take the first step toward looking for a more suitable job. She thinks and thinks but does not do anything about it.

Rachel gets nervous when the boss is around and worries that she might make a mistake. She is afraid he might get mad if she messes up. There are occasions when he even belittles her with foul language in front of other employees. She utters no words in her defense because she desperately wants his approval—which never comes.

So, let's pause here and look at this fictitious scenario. We need to look to her past to understand why Rachel behaves as passively as she does. Imagine that she comes from a dysfunctional family. What if her father was a tall, thin man who abused alcohol and was prone to verbal outbursts? And to make things more complicated, what if Rachel's abusive boss looked just like her father?

Finally, what if Rachel begins to recall childhood memories of her father verbally abusing her mother and the frightened look on her mom's face? She remembers how her mother remained still during those demeaning episodes. The mother didn't stand up for herself, leave the room, or say anything. She just stood there and took it. How might that childhood memory affect Rachel's submissive response to her bullying boss? Can you understand how seeing her boss standing over her and hearing him barking orders cause Rachel to regress emotionally to the habitual behavior she witnessed in childhood?

It's moments like this when I think of a porcupine's characteristics. The porcupine has quills that she uses to shield her when threatened. If a predator gets too hostile, the protective quills bristle up, and the porcupine is on guard. How great would it be if Rachel learned to tap into such defense mechanisms against the predatory personality of her boss? How might that change the situation?

If Rachel was your friend, you could suggest that she seek counseling and assertiveness skills training. Then, she might be better able to sit down with her boss and tell him how she feels about the way he treats her. However, the probability of her verbally abusive boss suddenly showing her understanding and compassion is nil. So, to be realistic, chances are her boss will remain disrespectful to her.

Since this is a made-up story, let's give it a happy ending by saying that Rachel learns to stand up for herself by utilizing the quills from her porcupine power. She realizes that she cannot force her boss to change. So, she practices assertiveness and takes positive action by finding another job. Thank goodness!

Today's Teaching from Mother Nature

Picture high waves on the ocean. The water's surface may look turbulent, but calmer waters are deep underneath it all. That's the way it is with your mind. You can find tranquility down deep in your soul. So, instead of ruminating, take positive action on whatever problem is on your mind. Let go of seeking approval, worrying about displeasing others, or fearing that you will make someone mad because of your decisions. Sit down and breathe slowly. Once you are calm, write out a plan. Then, follow through with your course of action. Do it today!

37
As Yielding as Running Water

When you struggle to have power over nature, it inevitably turns out to be an exercise in futility. It is akin to trying to resist a boulder rolling down a hill by stubbornly standing in front of it with your hand held out to stop it. You are going to get run over.

There is a more adaptive way to survive. Yield to the momentum of the boulder. You can go with the flow by running alongside the boulder and gently nudging it in a new direction. You can think of this action as resistance through nonresistance because you are not trying to stop the boulder completely; you only need to redirect it. Resistance is a type of response. Nonresistance involves limited participation, not unconditional surrender.

Take a lesson from water. Water has mastered the art of nonresistance through yielding. It may be soft but can wear down almost any hard substance over time. In human terms, this means that the soft, loving word is more powerful in the long run than the hard, cold word. In business, an inflexible policy will inevitably break if the challenge is too great, while the yielding policy can bend and adapt to change.

When you walk through a grassy field, notice how tall, dry grass is brittle and inflexible. It quickly breaks if you try to bend it. Conversely, when you examine a living blade of green grass, you can see how yielding it is as it bends. It is flexible and adaptive. Metaphorically, people who are rigid and refuse to bend will break like dead grass. People who *do* embrace life are flexible and can adjust to whatever challenges come along. The lesson Mother Nature teaches here is clear—either bend or break!

The idea of yielding through active nonresistance is a concept we may hear from time to time. However, it is one thing to know a concept and another thing to live it. That is why we should practice being as yielding and soft as water. Over time, we will succeed, so there is no need to force things to get done in a hurry. Resist the urge to be resistant. This is one of life's little paradoxes.

Incidentally, the art of active nonresistance is not just beneficial for individuals. It is also applicable in politics. When governments try to resist the people's will, leaders become overly controlling. Then, politicians forget about the public's best interests and focus on gaining power for themselves. The leaders need to loosen their controlling grip and give the citizens room to thrive.

Since you understand that nothing lasts forever, it is useless to resist the inevitable. Change is one of those inevitabilities. Far better it is to yield with poise than to stubbornly refuse to adapt until you snap like the dry grass. Eventually, everything transforms into something else. Just think how people could reduce their stress if they let go of their refusal to bend. You can accept the certainty of natural laws just as water yields to the flow of the current.

When you surrender to life, you can appreciate the richness of each moment. That includes the moment of death because death is part of life. The end of your life is a process of letting go. This process is not just about letting go of people, places, and things; it is also about letting go of your body. No resistance. When you learn to yield to the unavoidable, a cloak of peacefulness comes over you like a warm blanket. When you live life to the fullest, you feel complete and ready for the conclusion of your life cycle.

This idea of yielding to the flow reminds me of the last time I traveled by airplane. There were delays and weather conditions that were out of my control. Finally, I just yielded to the situation and decided to enjoy the adventure of the unexpected. As it turns out, I did have control over one thing—my attitude.

Have you ever tried to hold too many things in your grasp at one time and ended up dropping everything? That is what it's like trying to control everything around you. It all comes crashing down. Just let things flow naturally. Instead of micromanaging, trust that things will work out in the end. Trust does not mean you cannot oversee a project. Just don't breathe down their necks. You will find that this flexible approach inspires creativity in people. Once that happens, the people you work with can feel free to open their minds and let intuition take them down new paths, leaving behind fixed concepts and rigid rules.

Opening the mind to new ideas is an invitation for change. Change is sometimes scary because it deals with uncertainty, like stepping into darkness. However, when you have the light of love in your heart to guide you, you are connected to the Source of light, so there is nothing to fear. Carry on.

Today's Teaching from Mother Nature

It is time to put this yielding approach into practice. Everything has its flow. Please step back and allow your plans, work projects, and life to run their natural courses. Let the energy flow freely. Just as there is no need to push the river, you do not need to force things to their completion. Nor do you need to press others to speed through their activities. The more you try to control people, the more they will become defensive against your attempts to dominate. Be like running water—yield to the river of life.

38
Bad Dog! You Remind Me of Myself

One chilly fall day, I looked out the window and noticed my dog on the lawn. She was gnawing on an old, dry bone she'd craved for over a year. I couldn't imagine why my dog would still chew on an old bone that no longer had meat on it, yet she returned to it time and time again.

I realized I do the same thing with my outdated, unhealthy habits. Like a dog returning to an old bone, I tend to get caught up in long-standing, destructive patterns of thinking and behaving. Sometimes, those familiar habits feel like I'm slipping on a pair of worn-out slippers; they are comfortably tattered yet full of holes and lack practical use.

The bone in this story represents hollow desires. One example of a hollow desire is when people who suffer from addiction repeatedly return to the object of their addiction, even though it is not healthy for them or those around them. It doesn't matter what type of addiction; it could be alcohol, drugs, internet, junk food, pornography, and so on. All addictive cravings seem like a pile of dry bones. So, where is the nutrition?

Having an unhealthy habit is like wearing a leash, and the addictive behaviors can very quickly get that leash wrapped around trouble. This image reminds me of yet another behavior I witnessed my dog doing in the yard. When I put my dog on a long leash tied around a tree's trunk, she started circling the tree in the same direction and got all wrapped up. When she could go no farther, she whimpered and kept pulling on the leash as if she didn't know what else to do. If my dog just stopped resisting and relaxed, she would unwind. As it was, she was literally all wrapped up with no place to go.

I remember watching this display of canine futility and thinking how stupid it was for my dog not to realize that she needed to turn around and go in the opposite direction. Instead, she kept pulling in a pointless attempt to proceed in the same old way. That's when it struck me that I can be just as stupid when falling into my old, repetitive, impulsive habits.

Sometimes, I get all wrapped up in my problems because I keep going in the same misguided direction and cannot see another way. To change my former dysfunctional ways, I need accurate information and wisdom. I need to stop fighting and let my mind be peaceful. Then, I can finally unwind and be free of that controlling leash.

Hypothetically speaking, let's say a man named Charlie needed to handle his impulsive gambling and regain control over his life. His gambling started with pull tabs in bars; then, he progressed to casinos. Having experienced some modest wins, he quickly got hooked on the thrill of winning. He loved the way it made him feel when he won. It didn't matter how much; any win would put him in a good mood—at least temporarily. It got to the point where the mere thought of winning caused him to feel a sense of excitement. Even if the odds were against him, the possibility that he *could* win was enough to get his mind fixated on gambling. Then, before he knew what had happened, he found himself at the nearest casino.

Instead of judging Charlie for having weak willpower, let's be mindful that he is suffering and view him with compassion. We understand that we do not have the power to take away his addiction, so we provide what we have—deep listening and understanding. In his case, we can also refer him to a clinic that deals explicitly with gambling addiction.

Today's Teaching from Mother Nature

Look at others through the eyes of compassion because you don't always know what they are going through in life. They may be suffering from some form of addiction. If so, they need your understanding, not your condemnation. Remember, you do not need to fix their problems for them. Humbly provide emotional support and listen with a caring attitude.

If, on the other hand, *you* are the one struggling with addictive behaviors or simply trying to break an old habit, let go of those things that no longer serve you by mentally releasing the desires. Drop the old, dry bones, maladaptive habits, and dysfunctional relationships that do not have any benefits. Letting things go is the key. How do you let go? One of the best ways is to realize that dysfunctional behaviors are not worth hanging on to because those old habits have no nutrition in their bones. If you believe that you need treatment for your addiction, please get in touch with a local treatment center right away.

39

That Clingy Bug on My Windshield

Sometimes, people can be stubborn and cling to old, dysfunctional behaviors. Even though they know it's better to let go and adjust to the new situation, they seem stuck in their obstinate ways. Maybe as children, they started developing a willful personality trait. It probably seemed cute and precocious at that age, but it interferes with their ability to cope with everyday life as adults.

This maladaptive behavior is reminiscent of an insect I noticed on my car windshield as I pulled out of a parking lot. As I slowly headed down the side street, the insect didn't know when to let go, so it kept hanging on. The longer it stayed, the faster my car traveled. Pretty soon, I was on the highway going so fast that the poor thing flew off with the next bump in the road. It would've been more prudent for that little bug to let go several minutes earlier, but it didn't pick up on the cues. It didn't know when to call it quits. People sometimes do this, too. It's not until they hit a bump that they are thrown into the reality of their situation.

Listen, I trust you are a good person with compassion for others. Even so, you must care for yourself before showing compassion to someone else. So, what signs indicate that your behavior may need a slight adjustment? How do you know when your conduct crosses the line from unusual to dysfunctional? When do your quirky personality traits become problematic?

Let me start by stating that no personality type is better than another. There is a need for every kind of person in our society, including introverts, extroverts, feeling-orientated types, tech aficionados, social butterflies, empathic individuals, risk-takers, sensitive people, and so on. We all have a place in the world and are all emotionally interconnected on a human level. Without those individuals who pay attention to every little detail, we wouldn't have precise computer software. Conversely, if we didn't have people who could step back and see the big picture, we wouldn't have architects and engineers who conceptualize, organize, and construct plans for massive projects.

So, what's the tipping point? When are you being like that bug on the windshield that stubbornly refused to let go? How can you assess whether you have crossed the line into maladaptive behavior? Well, being sensitive to your feelings, for instance, is acceptable. However, if your sensitivity makes you too anxious to be around other people, that is the tipping point. Feeling down when it is a cold and rainy day is one thing, but feeling so depressed you cannot get out of bed for days is crossing the line into dysfunctional behavior. Furthermore, being so distracted by the side conversations around you that you cannot concentrate is also problematic.

There is yet another personality type that, like the insect, seems to have great difficulty letting go of things. These individuals don't know when to drop an issue. They keep talking long after others have grown tired of listening to them. They seem to cling to something that bothers them and cannot let it go. I bet you can think of someone who doesn't know when to shut up.

Determining whether the behavior is simply different or dysfunctional can be very confusing. Let me try to pull it all together as simplistically as I can. There is nothing inherently dysfunctional about being different or unusual, even eccentric. However, when behaviors, thoughts, or emotions interfere with your ability to function in some significant area of your life, it is a red flag that those things are becoming problematic.

Just because you are unhappy with some aspects of your life does not necessarily mean you are completely incompetent. However, suppose you are incapable of enjoying life or unable to cope with essential responsibilities. In that case, that issue is worth your attention and needs further investigation by a qualified professional. Remember, this does not mean every little quirky behavior you have requires you to rush in for a mental health evaluation. This information is merely a guideline.

Your general behavior is probably okay if you can cope effectively with everyday challenges. Everyone is unique, and that's a beautiful thing. Enjoy your individuality. At the same time, recognize when your behaviors, thoughts, and emotions become problematic. Understand the difference between unconventional and pathological.

We all know that each wave on a lake consists of water. Therefore, one wave is no better than another, nor does one wave feel inferior. Likewise, no person needs to feel inferior to anyone else. On a higher vibrational level, all our energy is one. (Oh, don't look at me like that; you know what I mean.)

Today's Teaching from Mother Nature

Take a slow, deep breath and do a little self-reflection. Are you able to perform all your daily functions mindfully and safely? If so, congratulations. If not, you might want to dig deeper to find out what's going on. Are there some maladaptive behaviors you have that disrupt your ability to function in life? Are there some habitual thoughts you have that interfere with your enjoying life to the point you cannot cope very well?

The answers to these questions may determine whether your behavior is simply different or dysfunctional. With good self-awareness, if you feel you would benefit from counseling, please seek the assistance of a mental health provider. Love yourself enough to ask for help. Don't be like the obstinate insect on the windshield that refuses to act promptly. You need to care for yourself before you can adequately care for others.

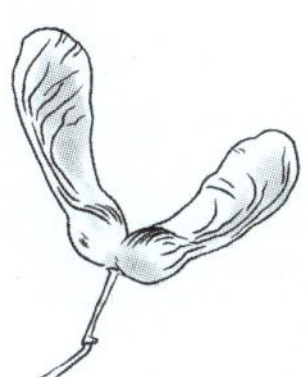

40
Morals Between a Bobcat and a Fawn

Let's be frank; we feel angry when our ethics are violated. From that standpoint, anger is a moralistic emotion. Think about it. We become angry when we believe the other person is wrong and we are right. And if we were hurt somehow, then of course we think that calls for retaliation. Rage is very self-righteous because it makes someone else a bad character.

What if, for instance, you witness a parent scolding a child in a store? As the small child starts to cry loud enough for the whole store to hear, you feel your anger welling up. You disagree with this punitive parenting style and believe the parent to be wrong because that is not how *you* might handle the situation. However, there is another way of viewing such life events. What if you took the perspective that there is no absolute correct way of doing things? What if no one was to blame? When you suspend judgment, there is no need to place blame. Then what happens to the anger? It evaporates like the morning mist in the dawn's sunlight.

Now, if the situation were extreme and the parent became violent and started abusing the child, you are morally obligated to intervene and contact the police. However, even in such an extreme case, you could keep your cool and act without anger. Losing your temper and venting your anger on another person is simply counterproductive. When you stay in control of yourself, you are more rational.

My moralistic anger was put to the test one spring day by none other than Mother Nature Herself! There was a mother bobcat with her kittens who lived in the woods just beyond my backyard. As the bloodred sun was in the colorful evening sky, I heard a fawn crying at the edge of the woods because the mother bobcat was taking him down. I angrily shouted at the bobcat and scared her off. Upon closer inspection, the fawn had only suffered a small bite on one of his hind legs and, in a few seconds, could still get up and run to safety.

At first, I felt proud of myself for saving the life of the fawn. However, when I later pondered the incident during meditation, I realized I had taken a meal away from the mother bobcat and her kittens. The bobcat was only doing what Mother Nature had designed her to do. She can only live by eating other animals. By interfering with nature's design, I quite literally had taken food out of the mouths of those poor kittens, who, no doubt, went hungry that night.

Next time, I will let nature take its course and not interfere or inflict my morality on other beings. The lesson Mother Nature taught me that day was to let go of insisting on *my* will and, instead, accept the will of *nature*. Reflecting on my thoughts, emotions, and behavior, it seems illogical for me to have gotten so angry with the mother bobcat for not living up to my *human* morals.

Perhaps, like me, you get angry when others do not live up to your morals and expectations. When was the last time you became enraged at someone? Review the situation in your mind. In retrospect, can you see how at least part of your anger resulted from someone not meeting your standards? Where is it written that people must live by *your* rules? Is it your mission in life to be a faultfinder? Although you still may feel disappointed when people make poor decisions, you do not have to heap blame on them.

From a different point of view, anger can be seen as a mask to cover up hurt feelings or fear. Sometimes, you may not want to admit being scared or emotionally wounded, especially if you feel vulnerable after being verbally rebuked. In such a case, anger can be a defense mechanism when you think you are under attack. It's a form of self-preservation.

If you step back and take a broader perspective, fear is almost always at the root of anger. Imagine, for example, a situation where you come home incredibly late without calling, and your family is angry with you. Their anger is about the fear that you were possibly hurt or in some trouble. Worry may come across as anger or even rage. When that happens, that type of rage can be a primal behavior. So, when you lose your temper and scream, you instinctually respond like a wild animal.

What can be done to control anger outbursts? I learned to let go of my anger by no longer placing value on it. I recognize that anger will not bring me the inner peace I seek. The same goes for guilt and hatred, too. In short, anger takes me farther away from tranquility, not closer.

One of the great things about being human is that we can choose our thoughts. Furthermore, we decide what meaning to ascribe to an event. Events, by themselves, have no intrinsic meaning. We decide what to make of it, positive or negative. If you want to be negative and interpret every comment you hear as rude, you will be offended daily, leading to anger and hatred. On the other hand, if you look for good intent in every comment, you can give a positive meaning to the words you hear. With that type of attitude, you are much more likely to feel happier and much less likely to get upset.

I choose to give a positive meaning to everything that happens to me. At times, I do feel the emotion of anger at first. But then, I look for the positive in the situation. As a result, I feel happier. For me, everything in life is a learning experience. Then, even a so-called bad thing becomes something from which to learn.

On a deeper level, every life experience has something about it from which you can learn. And yes, you learn from your relationships with others. Therefore, you can look forward to the new things you will learn from the next person you meet.

Today's Teaching from Mother Nature

Before you fall asleep tonight, think about the mother bobcat and the crying fawn. Realize that Mother Nature made creatures to live and behave in a certain way, not necessarily according to *your* morals.

Now, instead of wild animals, focus your mind on humans. Think of at least one person with whom you are angry. Review your original reasons for believing this person was wrong. Was it because that person was not living up to your expectations? Recognize that anger is a moralistic emotion. Your belief that the other person is wrong contains thoughts of self-righteousness. Let go of the tendency to focus only on the negative qualities of that person and focus on the positive ones as well. Now forgive that person and have a peaceful night's sleep.

41

As Diligent as a Bird Building a Nest

When you have great ambition, one of the best ways to transcend beyond a basic idea to its full manifestation is to flow with the project's momentum without forcing it to completion. If you've ever watched a bird build a nest, you understand how a big job needs to be broken down into smaller parts. When that happens, your work goes smoother. And when you get into the rhythm of your work, it doesn't feel like work anymore. It's achieving without all the pressure and stress, doing something without the labor burden.

During one spring season, I watched with amazement as a bird gradually built her nest in a pine tree outside my kitchen window. Every morning, as I ate my breakfast, I observed the natural progression of the bird's steady work. Her effort was smooth and flowing as if she were not even trying.

At first, the bird started with a few long pieces of dried grass. Slowly, the nest grew as she brought in more material, including mud. As the days progressed, the nest became bigger and thicker. When the bird's work was completed, she had a beautiful home for her and her mate to raise a little family. What seemed at first to be a daunting task was handled with ease by taking things one step at a time.

Similarly, you, too, can transcend and exceed the aspirations in your life by diligently working at it daily. The trick is to start that big job when it is still small and manageable. Do not wait until the problem becomes large and overwhelming. When you have the mindset that a series of small steps can help you achieve great things, you can accomplish without trying hard. You do not need to force anything.

As you are flowing toward your goals, make sure you avoid certain stumbling blocks. I would be remiss if I did not express caution here about when to stop and let go. How do you know when enough is enough? You do not want to overreach your purpose. To excel and move forward is fine. However, don't get greedy and push things too far where everything unravels and falls apart.

Think of it this way: That cute bird constructed her nest just big enough to accommodate her family, no larger. She did not keep on building and building until the nest could fit a basketball. I think it's fair to say that the bird had no intention of laying an ostrich egg! She knew when to stop; she knew the limits. Do you?

Even the labels we use to describe ourselves and others have limits. Let's refer to those limits as expiration dates. Consider the self-descriptive terms we use as children, such as *baby*, *kid*, *teenager*, or *young adult*. Do those terms still apply? These categories we use to define ourselves change over time as we transcend them. They are provisional. Therefore, we need to know when to stop using outdated classifications so they do not hold us back. If we want to produce wonderful things as the nesting birds do, we should transcend restrictive labels.

Just as with labels, another stumbling block exists with societal roles. Whatever function you currently have, that role can also be restrictive and limit your ability to flow and grow. Understand that any position you have will ultimately come to an end. Nothing is permanent; nothing stays the same. Although your role may serve a purpose here and now, it will eventually cease or at least transform. You can avoid many a stumble by having the wisdom to transcend your role when it no longer leads you closer to personal development and emotional wellness.

Along the same lines, knowing how to move past an issue and prevent a problem from getting out of hand is essential. When a problem is new, it is easy to adjust. Therefore, be more proactive and stop problems before they grow bigger so you can remain productive and fulfill your purpose. And part of sidestepping these stumbling blocks involves leaving the aggression out.

I do not think all problems are destructive. It can be healthy to work on an issue without battling it. In other words, work on the solution instead of fighting the problem. Specifically, the aggressive element of conflict inherently brings destructive qualities, such as anger, rage, bitterness, resentment, and spite.

Having said that, if someone is trying to start a fight, you do not need to engage with that person. If the energy of the situation is too negative, sometimes the best option is not to get involved in the struggle. Remember, if you refuse to fight, the opponent is no longer your competitor. When you do not feed energy into the battle, the opponent may leave and look for trouble elsewhere. This shrewd technique is one way to sidestep conflict and reach your aspirations.

Today's Teaching from Mother Nature

Take a minute to sit down and reflect upon a bird building a nest. Now, with the diligence of that bird, write out one of your aspirations. It doesn't matter which one. Once you have your purpose defined clearly, break it down into smaller chunks. That way, it's easier to manage.

When difficulties arise, as they must, do not resist reality or get angry. Instead of fighting, work with the flow and turn the situation into something enjoyable. When you let go of your restrictive labels, limiting roles, and aggressive behavior, troubles will be no trouble. When you have reasonable success and sense things have run their course, stop and let things be as the nesting birds do.

42
Be a Pillar, Not a Caterpillar

Words, words, words. There is certainly no shortage of opinions these days. It seems everyone has something to say. The question is, who's listening? Where are the people who lead by example? Some billionaires can buy social status with smooth talk and generous charitable contributions—all tax deductible, of course. But what is beyond that? Is there anything deeper? Do people practice what they preach anymore? Responsible people do not just talk about improving the community—they go out and do it!

When I think about this topic, I imagine a large stone building with tall pillars. I see the tiny caterpillars moving about aimlessly on the granite floor. The pillars provide a useful purpose by supporting the structure. The caterpillars, on the other hand, don't do much at all. They only crawl in and crawl out. People in positions of authority need to learn how to be pillars, not caterpillars. (Yes, you have my permission to use this metaphor at your next staff meeting.)

People can learn by seeing your work's success and naturally want the same results. They may ask questions regarding how you did it. You can serve them best at times like this by letting them discover solutions independently. You do not need to tell them precisely what to do because you do not want them to follow your instructions mindlessly without thinking for themselves. On the contrary, you want to encourage them to discover answers independently. In other words, foster independence.

Set a precedent for your neighborhood and demonstrate a caring attitude. Let the twinkle of kindness shine in your eyes. You may be surprised at what you can accomplish when this compassion is in your heart. Remember, there is nothing you must prove; you do not need to convince anyone. People will either follow your lead or not. Their approval is not a requirement for your positive attitude. Conversely, you do not need to be judgmental or reject anyone just because their ways are not yours. Each person has a path to walk through life, and so do you. The essential thing is that you walk your talk.

No one can force another to be happy because happiness comes from within the individual. People may comment that they want to marry someone who will make them happy for the rest of their lives. Sound familiar? If people are unhappy, no one else can bring happiness to them on a silver platter. Similarly, you cannot make people live according to your ethical standards. It just doesn't work. That is why it is best to be a supportive pillar and serve as a role model. You may have already found that imposing your will on others is counterproductive.

And while we are on the subject, let's have a word of caution about being preachy. No one likes being preached to or belittled; it's patronizing. A simple way to avoid this pitfall is to let Mother Nature be your model. When it storms, the wind blows, and it eventually passes. Then, things are quiet and still. The storm does not go on and on endlessly. Let your words be like the blowing wind and rain. Say what you need to say. Then, let the wind from your mouth be quiet and still, like after a storm. Your actions will speak louder than words.

If a loved one is on a self-destructive path and will not follow your guidance, it can feel very frustrating. Sometimes, events must run their natural course for a person to learn valuable life lessons. When these painful times occur, stay grounded in your principles. One way to do this is to imagine that you are in the center of a protective bubble.

The bubble is safe and warm and allows you to see what is happening outside the sphere without being emotionally overwhelmed by the chaotic situation. Try this visualization out and see how it works for you.

Eventually, the hardship will pass, then your loved one can see life more clearly. That person will trust you more as time passes because you have no ulterior motives. Your words can be trusted when you have no hidden agenda to push. Your actions are consistent, and this consistency eventually builds trust.

We all stumble and fall. We can view failure as an opportunity to learn and grow. When we compromise our principles and fall short of our standards, it is vitally important to fess up to what we did (or didn't do). We do not need to look for someone to blame because doing so creates a vicious circle. Once that old blame game starts, it is hard to stop. Instead, we can take accountability for our words and actions. Then, we are ready to amend our mistakes.

Today's Teaching from Mother Nature

The next time you go out in public, be a supportive pillar and set a good example by showing kindness and courtesy to those you meet. It is not difficult and does not have to be a grand spectacle. It can be as simple as holding the door open for someone. Then, watch the positive energy spread. Your example may catch on, and you may notice someone else holding the door for another person coming in!

Remember, what you are doing speaks louder than what you are saying. This phenomenon also works well in traffic jams. Maybe you witnessed one driver kindly allowing another to merge into a lane. And when the other drivers saw this example of politeness, they started to show the same considerate behavior. Courtesy, indeed, is contagious! So be the best pillar you can be.

43

Don't Tug on Plants to Hurry Growth

Sometimes, when people lose confidence in their ability to manage themselves, they depend on an establishment to solve their problems. In their dependent futility, people stop trusting themselves and turn to authority figures who are often drunk with power.

Moreover, when people want to escape from the discomfort of thinking for themselves and are struggling with tough philosophical questions, they may rely on the preexisting beliefs from any number of extremist religions and cults. These radical organizations seem to have ready-made answers for their followers. Consequently, they teach conformity and submission, not compassion and patience.

Perhaps we all need to take a second look and reexamine our life situation. Do we need to be told what to do and how to live our lives? Is there another way to find answers? Maybe we could be teachers to ourselves and discover some of those answers independently without worshipping at the altar of codependency.

Is simplicity part of your belief system, or do you tend to make your life much more complicated than it needs to be? Following simple steps with clear thoughts can lead to outstanding accomplishments with relative ease. Just being in the moment is a good way to enjoy the simplicity of life. One way to do this is by going on a meditative walk. This involves focusing on every step, sound, and smell around you as you walk. It also calls for a keen inner sense of what is happening inside your body, like sensations, emotions, and thoughts.

When it comes to compassion, people need to realize that it starts with themselves. All too often, people try so hard to teach compassion to someone else, all while neglecting their own needs in the process. It's as if they forget about self-care. If people do not know how to be kind to themselves, they certainly cannot teach kindness to anyone else.

As for teaching patience, show acceptance to those you like *and* to those you do not prefer. This is a true test of your tolerance level. Can you see past the petty differences and squabbles to find common ground? Do you have the resolve to wait for the right moment to come to you instead of constantly chasing after it like a cat dashing for a flashlight beam moving across the floor?

Being patient with yourself and others also means not interfering with the natural order, just like you wouldn't try to pry open the buds on the trees in the springtime. Let things happen naturally. The farmer does not need to impatiently go into her field and tug on the plants to make them grow faster. What good would that do? That irrational behavior would only ruin the crops. However, when the farmer is patient, she teaches tolerance to those around her by being a positive role model.

We all have much more to learn, no matter how smart we think we are. It is beneficial to the learning process to be humble. After all, if we believe we know it all, our minds are closed to learning anything new. To acknowledge that we still have much to understand is to open ourselves up to new possibilities. These new possibilities can lead to greater independence, allowing us to manage our lives better.

If a man or woman wants to be a leader, that person would do well first to become a teacher. A true leader will guide, not dictate. Here again, simplicity is a valuable commodity. And the most effective teachers are the ones who keep it simple. Simplicity is clarity; isn't that what people want? Seeking clarity is natural. Therefore, you can teach by guiding people back to their true nature. Doesn't that make sense?

Let us not forget that our critics can be some of our best teachers. Think about it. It is unlikely our friends will criticize our mistakes. However, our adversaries sure will. And that's okay because we can learn from our opposition. Think of them as blunt friends without social skills.

Imagine having a blunt boss with the ill-mannered personality of a disgruntled buffalo. What if she criticized your work every day? At first, it bothered you. But then, you realized she had a point. With some self-reflection, you learned from her unpleasant remarks and used them to improve yourself. Granted, you were not excusing her rude behavior. You just figured that she must have graduated from the same charm school as a drill sergeant.

When you teach others, you do not want to force your will on them. You can teach a great deal by just modeling positive behavior. Instead of meddling, you can let them struggle for a while. This can be a valuable learning tool. They will gain knowledge from experience, especially the mistakes. Sometimes, you can step aside, let nature run its course, and trust that life can be the best teacher.

Just as a fire burns itself out when it no longer has fuel, things such as arguments, anger, negative thoughts, and destructive emotions extinguish when you stop feeding them energy. Patience pays off, and compassion is stronger than hatred. It's interesting how giving up intolerance brings about patience. The loss of one can give birth to the other.

Today's Teaching from Mother Nature

Picture in your mind a farmer in her field. She has the wisdom to be patient and wait for the crops to grow. She does not try to stretch the plants by tugging them, hoping they will grow quickly. Ponder on this wisdom. To be more patient with others, you must be patient with yourself first. If you genuinely want to be compassionate, you should care enough to teach others how to improve their lives. Put plainly, teach compassion and patience.

44
Transforming into a Butterfly

Chances are you probably avoid discomfort at all costs. However, that cost can be high because you lose the opportunity to grow from that challenging experience. Learning how to walk as a toddler was a difficult experience, yes? Can you imagine what your life would be like if you'd avoided the discomfort of that challenge? You would probably still be crawling around on all fours.

Think of the benefits you could receive by effectively dealing with your discomfort and rising to the challenge. You could become happier than ever before. So, what personal transformation do you want most? What is stopping you from reaching that goal? Could it be you are avoiding the discomfort involved in achieving that objective? You know it will take hard work. Is that what's holding you back?

All of us benefit from a healthy amount of self-discipline. However, we do not need to be so overly scheduled and self-monitoring that we lose our natural spontaneity and creativity. We need that balanced level of self-control that allows us to look past the hard work and see the grand prize that awaits us after our transformation.

Think about the transformation that takes place with a butterfly pupa (chrysalis) struggling to emerge from a cocoon. The would-be butterfly tussles to break free from its casing and benefits from the effort made. If the pupa didn't work so hard, it would not develop the strength necessary to survive later in life. The comparison is clear; people also need to put in adequate effort to experience transformation in life.

Take the fictional case history of someone we will call Toni. She was a middle-aged single woman with no job and, seemingly, no ambition. Typically, she stayed in bed until noon and made no effort to maintain her living environment. So many dishes needed washing that they no longer fit in the sink and had to be scrubbed in the bathtub. The laundry pile was so high she could almost ski down the mound. To top it all off, there was so much clutter on the floor she could twist her ankle trying to walk across the living room.

Just for dramatic effect, let's pretend that she also had a very young daughter and that the home situation was so bad she risked losing custody of her only child because of parental neglect. Essentially, the child was raising herself. On many occasions, the little girl arrived at her elementary school in the morning with an empty stomach because she did not get any breakfast at home. To make matters worse, the mother often neglected to pack a lunch for her child to take to school.

Toni's only activity was watching television, which she did all day and all night. She often slept in the reclining chair parked in front of the TV to avoid missing any of her shows. Her phone was always within reach so she could order fast food instead of cooking. Then, when the delivery person knocked at the door, she hollered, "The door is open!" That way, she didn't need to get up from watching TV, and the bags of food were delivered to her lap. It seemed her whole purpose in life was to avoid any discomfort. Consequently, her life had no personal growth or positive transformation without the challenges accompanying discomfort.

Now, let's make up a happy ending to this story of extreme lethargy. To create a positive transformation, let's imagine that Toni received counseling and eventually learned the lesson of the emerging nymph butterfly. Mainly, she learned there was value in putting forth an effort toward a worthy goal. Once she realized there was something to gain from the effort, something she wanted badly, she enrolled in college and gave her life and her daughter's life a meaningful purpose. (Aww, I love happy endings.)

Like our fictional friend, Toni, we all need a purpose in life that gives us the strength to work through the struggle and leads us to transformation. If we avoid exertion, we miss out on growth. We can't have it both ways. Trying to accomplish a meaningful goal without facing the inherent labor in the attainment of said goal doesn't pan out. Far too often, our mindset is to try and reap the rewards of hard work without doing the labor required; that is a self-defeating attitude.

Reflecting on how continued effort leads to personal development, I contemplate how physical exercise can lead to good health. I have engaged in moderate exercise my whole life, even in childhood. I jokingly tell my friends that when my mother was pregnant with me and had an ultrasound, the image showed me doing pull-ups from one of her ribs.

Realistically, I am not talking about being a star athlete or anything like that. I only do a few push-ups and sit-ups at home and daily walks. The exercise is nothing too strenuous, yet I have repeatedly reaped the rewards of good health. It is an incredible sensation to be physically fit. I could never have achieved this state of fitness if I avoided the work of exercising. I look at it this way: I need to take care of my body because I have nowhere else to live!

I think of the busy beavers when it comes to achieving through effort. Over the years, I observed them building dams on the creek near my home. So, I understand the relentlessness with which they labor. They are not in a hurry, nor are they stressed out. They keep at it until they complete the job. Where would the beavers be if they spent their time swimming away from work? I'll tell you where; they'd be homeless!

Today's Teaching from Mother Nature

Nature knows best. Go outdoors and observe the lessons the animals can teach you every day. Notice the birds gathering twigs for their nests, the spider in the corner busily spinning a web, and the pupa struggling to emerge from the cocoon as a butterfly. All are labors of love. You can start to view challenges excitedly because you now understand that diligent work will inevitably transform into personal growth.

45

Hawks Can Teach You Mindfulness

In what areas of your life would you like to experience more success? What about your psychological well-being, physical health, career, finances, recreational activities, personality improvements, attitude adjustments, social skills, and so on? Can you picture yourself flourishing in all these areas? How would you look? What expression would you have on your face?

You may have your own style for completing your goals. However, it might be beneficial to discuss some new ideas because fresh concepts can give you a novel way of viewing things. It's like having a unique angle when looking at a beautiful sunrise; you appreciate the colors, skyline, and trees silhouetted against the brilliant backdrop of the morning rays completely differently.

Many of us have heard that hard work pays off. This tends to be accurate, especially if done mindfully. Why? Because working in a state of awareness moves us gradually closer toward success. Interestingly, humans are not the only ones who benefit from staying focused on goals. Hawks, too, can teach us a thing or two about accomplishments.

One day, on a daily walk, I noticed a female hawk rising from a meadow. The hawk seemed to put forth a lot of energy getting off the ground. She intensely flapped her wings as she made a large, upward spiral pattern toward the sky. She was mindful enough to catch the higher air currents above the trees and rode the wind calmly. Stretching out her wings, she soared effortlessly across the blue sky.

It struck me how the hawk's situation applies to humans. Hawks can soar after working hard to reach a place high enough that allows them to glide. Sometimes, we, too, need to put in much effort at the beginning of a project to get the ball rolling. Staying mindful and focused, we slowly rise to a higher level of progress. Once we have reached our goal, we can metaphorically stretch out our wings and soar while enjoying the benefits of our labor.

What if you had an out-of-shape friend who needed to do something immediately to tone his muscles? He understood that his sedentary lifestyle was putting him at risk for several potential problems down the road if he didn't improve his physical condition. Imagine that this friend sought your counsel regarding how to get back in shape.

After a physical exam from his physician, she told him it was okay to start exercising. So, the two of you worked on setting some realistic fitness goals. You also devised a plan of action to reach those goals within a practical timeline. Over the next several months, that action plan started to work for him, and he was eventually able to get physically fit.

This same approach can work for you, too, in the pursuit of any goal. You can have a life by *choice* rather than a life by *chance*. So, how do you get your hard work to pay off? Here are some friendly suggestions.

Start by figuring out what unmet need you have in your life. Typically, this is an emotional need. If you dig down deeply, you will discover underneath all those superficial wants is an emotional need trying to express itself. One of the strongest emotional needs is to give and receive love.

Make it your goal to satisfy that deep emotional need. Look beyond the superficial desire for material possessions and address the emotions behind the issue. You may, for instance, say you want a great deal of money. But what emotional need are you trying to satisfy with that money? It might be the desire for security, power, freedom, or some other strong need.

Make a written plan with specific steps to bring you gradually closer to achieving your goal. Give yourself a reasonable amount of time. Be patient.

Now it is time to act! All those plans you made can only work if you put them into practice. It is not enough to only stare at the goal you wrote down. Look at the steps in your plan and start doing them individually. Remember, it will take effort and endurance to complete your goal. You have the rest of your life to live, so pace yourself.

It also helps to be realistic when setting and working toward your goals with humility. Once again, another hawk exemplified this behavior as I traveled a country road one day. I saw a hawk flying toward the top of a power pole. When he came just a few feet away from reaching the pole, he made a sudden downward swoop as if on a roller coaster. Then, like a rocket, he swung up to the top of the pole, where he came to rest and perched.

From observing this hawk, I learned that when approaching the completion of a goal, it is good to be humble before reaching the top. Being wary of arrogance and overconfidence is wise. The best-laid plans in the world can be ruined just before completion if pride and complacency get in the way.

Today's Teaching from Mother Nature

Reflect on the character of hawks. Be mindful of the messages they are showing you in their behavior. Remember, the noble hawks can only soar after exerting effort, flapping their wings until high enough to ride the wind currents with composure gracefully. Metaphorically, you can do the same.

Additionally, be mindful of how hawks practice humility and dip down before rising to reach their goal of perching on a pole. How does this relate to your life? What message does the hawk have for you?

46
Take a Lesson from the Feisty Robins

Families can be a source of love and support, yet they can also be a source of hurt and suffering. To illustrate this point, I will create a story about a woman in her mid-thirties who was deeply troubled about being overly involved with her family of origin. While growing up, she experienced abuse repeatedly by her father. As an adult, she was torn between seeing him during family gatherings and needing to detach from him altogether.

She was strong enough to establish healthy boundaries with her family, but she couldn't decide on the limits. On the one hand, if she refused to see him, she would miss most family time, especially during holidays. On the other hand, she did not want to face her father because the memories of the childhood abuse were still fresh in her mind. Every time she saw him, she felt like a vulnerable child again, scared and needing protection.

When I think about this type of family scenario, it always brings back a memory of seeing a robin's nest in the sturdy branches of a large sugar maple in my front yard. I watched both parents flying back and forth, bringing worms and grubs to the hungry baby birds.

Suddenly, I heard a loud, sharp screeching sound coming from the edge of the woods. Turning my head, I saw a blue jay flying rapidly toward the robin's nest. With a flurry of flapping wings and fierce cries, both robins intercepted the threatening blue jay before it could harm the baby birds. With feathers flying and talons scratching, the robins drove the blue jay back into the woods and away from the nest. Then, the robins returned to the nest to ensure their babies were unharmed.

Which of those birds do you think the woman in the hypothetical scenario most closely identifies with? I'm guessing it's the robins, including the vulnerable babies and the protective parents. I bet those fragile little birds represented the scared and hurt child within her. It was her vulnerable side that she wanted to protect. It was stated earlier that when she was around her dad, she felt as though she was a small, weak child again. That's the part of her she wanted to guard by not seeing her father.

So, how is she also like the adult robins? Chances are she has a strong side to her personality that wants to protect her vulnerable inner child. The fact that she was willing to establish healthy boundaries with her family indicates that she was a strong defender. She can tap into this inner strength when needing to protect her inner child.

Okay, you've probably already guessed who the nasty blue jay is—her abusive father. He was always an imposing man who threatened her. How he stood before her and glared at her made her feel about two inches tall. He seemed to have power over her, the power to take away her confidence in a second.

So, let's tie all the loose ends together and wrap up this imaginary example. If the baby birds represent the part of her that is vulnerable and needs protection, the parent robins represent the part of her that is a defender, and the blue jay represents her abusive father. What lesson has Mother Nature taught you from this story?

Do you think she needs to chase away the blue jay and keep him far from her vulnerable side? Hell yes! She needs to protect her inner child from getting hurt, which means she must also protect her adult self. It might be a different situation if the father was actively engaged in family therapy or an anger management program. However, for this story, let's assume that the cruel father refuses to accept professional help for his dysfunctional behavior. In that case, for her well-being, she must have as little to do with her (still abusive) father as possible.

In reality, you or I may have had a different life scenario in which we acted differently than she did. However, the shared lesson for all of us is to stand up for ourselves and establish healthy, personal boundaries that protect our inner child and self-respect.

Today's Teaching from Mother Nature

Sit in quiet stillness and reflect upon the areas of your life that need healthier boundaries. Then, take positive and reasonable action, such as deciding how much involvement you want certain people to have in your life.

47

Sink Your Roots and Be Grounded

During your childhood, perhaps you tried to balance yourself while walking on one of the rails on the train tracks. With your arms out at your sides, the goal was to see how long you could go before needing to touch your foot down to rebalance yourself. Such is life. Sometimes, your journey is smooth and steady. At other times, you are wildly flailing about, trying not to fall on your rear. Balance in all things is the key to life.

In effect, the whole universe is trying to stay in balance. It's not just us. Everything in nature looks to be rebalanced when the forces are too strong in one area and not strong enough in another. Our bodies also strive for this type of homeostasis. It happens without us being aware of it. Therefore, when we maintain balance, we are in harmony with the universe's natural order. This harmony gives us more youthful energy. So, we had better enjoy our present age because today, we are younger than we will be tomorrow.

The world gives us so many mixed messages that losing our balance is easy. Then, we are out of touch with our true nature. One of the first telltale warning signs that we are getting out of balance is when we feel ourselves becoming restless. When this happens, we impulsively desire to leap first and look later. However, in such moments, we should slow down, take a deep breath, and reestablish an emotional equilibrium. Diaphragmatic breathing is one way to reconnect with our true nature.

Here is another way to stay centered. This one involves the use of a visualization technique. Imagine that your character is a strong, healthy tree. Visualize your toes turning into roots. Sink your roots deep into the rich soil of the earth. Picture your roots traveling down to the center of the planet. Wrap your roots around the core of Mother Earth and anchor yourself securely. This will help you feel grounded and steady.

With this new sense of stability, bring your mind's awareness to your upper body. Imagine your arms are strong and mighty tree limbs. Reach your branches to the sky. On the ends of your branches, visualize the old leaves falling off as fresh green leaves sprout to replace them. Let the sunshine fill those new leaves with the energy of life. You feel balanced and centered.

There are examples of lives out of balance all around us. Take, for instance, this imaginary case of a man unhappy with his life because he got laid off unexpectedly. He is in a loveless marriage, smokes heavily, and relieves stress by shouting at others. Several times a week, he spends the evening at the local bar trying to drink away his suffering, which only gets worse with each additional drink. He needs to rebalance his life.

His family had a heart-to-heart conversation with him, expressing their concern and encouraging him to seek professional help. (Okay, let's call it what it is—an intervention.) The man acknowledged that his life was spinning out of control. As part of his rebalancing act, he agreed to a reasonable behavioral plan involving daily relaxation exercises and mindfulness of how his emotions and actions affect those around him. These lifestyle changes brought his energy back into balance. It was not until he agreed to improve his life that he found the internal motivation to bring harmony back into his mind and soul.

Your body craves homeostasis. It is your biological nature to seek balance. You don't have to work at it. It's as easy as letting go of your stubbornness and allowing nature to take its course. Going with the harmonious flow of nature is not fighting; it's cooperating. And yet, people are fighting to find harmony and balance. They are on a misguided path. You cannot force your way into a state of harmony any more than you can order someone to have fun.

To illustrate this, let's return to the earlier image of the balancing act performed on the railroad tracks. When you lose your balance on the rail, you typically start waving your arms wildly as you desperately try to rectify yourself. Ironically, the more thrashing you do, the more you overextend yourself and fall. Put another way, trying too hard can throw you off balance.

So, how do folks know when their energies are in balance? Balanced people are typically reasonable in thought and action, are not emotionally bound to their ideas, and have patience with themselves and others. They are also flexible to change, view everything in life as an opportunity to learn, and care about the well-being of others.

Today's Teaching from Mother Nature

Write down all the significant areas of your life on paper. Are all these areas in balance with each other? If each of these items on your list were petals on a daisy, would some of those petals be missing, resulting in a lopsided flower? Is there a need for some adjustment? Let your energy be as homeostatic as the universe. Stay in balance by surrendering yourself to the wisdom of Mother Nature. That is the key to life.

48
The Fly and the Invisible Barrier

One summer day, I saw a fly in my house trying to escape through a closed window. The fly repeatedly hit against the glass, seemingly unable to find a way out. The glass had become an invisible barrier to freedom, imprisoning the fly. Attempting to assist, I opened the window to let the poor fly out. Surprisingly, the short-sighted fly did not recognize the new opening as a path to escape. It just continued its old ways of banging against the invisible obstruction. Finally, with some gentle nudging from me, it found the exit and ventured out into the world. (Whew!)

How often do we find ourselves in a similar predicament? For some reason, we cannot find our way out even though an alternative path may be right before us. This type of concrete thinking demonstrates an inability to think outside the box. We seem to lose the insight needed to come up with creative alternatives. So often, we have fixed concepts about how things should be or have always been.

It's as if we lock ourselves into only one perspective. And that perspective is usually our stubborn point of view. In our minds, our opinions become the truth as though they were facts. Then, we conclude that since our views are true for *us*, they must be true for *everyone*. So, of course, if anyone disagrees with our truth, that person must be wrong. And we all know that wrong people deserve punishment, right? Watch out! This type of thinking is how fanaticism, intolerance, and bigotry start.

Take religion, for example. (Yeah, that's a safe topic to discuss, right?) Your perception of the Creator was probably shaped to a large degree by fixed images and concepts that were handed down to you in childhood by your parents and religious leaders. In other words, your concepts about a Higher Power are most likely the result of religious programming and cognitive conditioning. You may wish to view yourself as someone who thinks independently, but let's face it, chances are you learned not to question those religious concepts, lest you be accused of losing faith and banished from the flock of devotees.

So here you are, still walking around with preconceived ideas about the Giver of Life that limit your mind's ability to see a broader perspective. Take a moment to do some personal reflection. What sort of limiting concepts do you have about the notion of a Higher Power? Do you think of the Creator as male? Why is that? Is that a reflection of your upbringing? Is your male deity concept based on ancient religious teachings and scriptures? If so, who wrote those scriptures—men, women, or both? Is it possible that the men who wrote, translated, and rewrote those scriptures had a gender bias in their favor?

So, how does all this affect how you think of men and women today? What role do you think men should play in our society? What about women? Are those roles different? Why is that? Where did you get those concepts? Are they limiting beliefs? Are those beliefs holding you back from progressing to a higher intellectual level?

Just as that fly on the window needed some gentle nudging to escape the invisible barrier, you, too, may need to seek out an open-minded sage. This knowledgeable guide may be able to give you a little nudge of encouragement to break free from those unseen and often unspoken conceptual barriers.

How do you know who a compatible mentor is for you? Your intuition will tell you. Let your inner wisdom guide you. Learn to listen to that soft voice inside of you. In time, the voice will grow stronger and more transparent.

Today's Teaching from Mother Nature

Find a quiet and private place in nature free from interruptions where you can sit down and do some introspective work. Any natural setting will do—the beach, woods, city park, a stream, or even your backyard. With your imagination, draw a protective circle around where you sit. Let your mind have a conversation with the Source of all life. You will be surprised how this experience broadens your mind. When you finish, remember to write about the lessons you have learned.

49
The Dark Kingdom of Your Mind

Some people say the awkwardness of meeting new people is the great beast of social life. Well, perhaps that beast is just misunderstood. Let's look deeper to uncover other things that might contribute to social discomfort. To do this, we need to seek an introspective view by asking ourselves soul-searching questions that can lead to a better understanding of others. Seeking answers, after all, is part of being human. It is our nature to search for reasons.

Typically, you might search for deep reasons in the universe by asking what life means. Well, maybe that's just it. Perhaps part of the meaning of life *is* to ask questions. Maybe we were made to seek answers. Keep in mind that finding answers often puts an end to an open mind. In other words, once you find an answer, you stop searching.

For instance, if you ask yourself a self-defeating question, such as why you don't socially fit in anywhere, then your mind may focus on how you are *different* from other people rather than *similar*. It is far better to concentrate on commonalities instead of differences. In short, if you focus on a negative question, you will get a negative answer, and you no longer search for additional information once you think you have the answer.

We need to keep an open mind. Otherwise, we stop learning and growing. For instance, some intolerant people hold bigoted beliefs and think we should not even dare to question their prejudice. But we have brains, so we question things, including social injustice. It is so ironic that our brains can question our questions. And that is precisely what I am asking you to do right now. I understand this is hard work, but when you are done, you can take a nap.

All this questioning and searching for self-understanding relates to our ability to feel interconnected with others. When we connect with a Higher Power, we bond with all creation. Connecting with Mother Nature is spiritually bridging with all the humans on Her planet. That's one way to relate and integrate.

Unfortunately, we don't always feel that sense of connection with others because we have some aspects of our past that we are not yet comfortable with. That area is the mental place where we keep our shameful secrets, a place I call the dark kingdom of the mind. We all have such a place, the corners of our souls, where we hide our dark thoughts and feelings. We hide these things because we think others would deem us unacceptable if they knew. After all, we don't like being rejected, misunderstood, or judged.

There are numerous examples of these shadowy secrets. However, let's focus on a common one—body image. Both women and men can struggle with insecurity issues of shame regarding their body image. Then, those shameful feelings can keep us from fully engaging in social interactions with the community. These negative emotions can very easily lead to withdrawal and social isolation. A negative self-image may very well be at the root of feeling like you don't fit in. In such a case, low self-esteem is usually the culprit.

That's just one of many examples. The point is, whatever your shame-based secrets may be, they are almost certainly interfering with your ability to feel emotionally connected to those around you. To be free from this mental prison, you must face the secrets of your dark kingdom. As a leaf flowing downstream breaks apart to pass through the logjams, you also can break apart your shame to pass through the blockage. Relaxation techniques like slow, deep breathing and guided imagery can help you release emotional logjams.

Working on overcoming the shameful secrets of the dark kingdom is analogous to a newborn pony struggling to stand on those wobbly legs. At first, the legs are unstable, but they soon grow more vigorous. For some odd reason, the image of the colt staggering to gain its footing always reminds me of the struggles people go through when trying to overcome chemical dependency.

Like that colt, people in recovery must do the work themselves with the help of their Higher Power and a licensed rehabilitation program. They should take an active role in breaking free from their dark kingdom—one day at a time. Putting forth the necessary effort is essential to strengthen those metaphoric wobbly legs.

At this point, I think it is necessary to address the issue of self-acceptance. Whether you are recovering from addiction or just struggling with the trials and tribulations of daily life, everybody has challenges. Many people are unhappy with who they are. They might think they would fit in and belong if they became more popular. You need to be comfortable with yourself before being comfortable with others. If you are not, others will have a more challenging time accepting you. People are quick to pick up on these insecurities. They may sense you are not confident in yourself, which may cause them to pull away from you.

Today's Teaching from Mother Nature

With an open mind, question your questions. We were made to question things and understand ourselves and others better. Therefore, in a social situation, don't just focus on yourself; try to meet the social needs of those around you, too. Be friendly, smile, and remember people are more likely to like you if you first like them! Most importantly, remember that everyone is human, and we all have a dark kingdom where we hide our secrets. In that way, you are just like them. So, you *do* fit in, after all!

50 Practical Lessons My Dog Taught Me

Nature provides what we need. That includes supplying practical metaphors, too. Our natural environment is a model for how we can conduct our lives. When we look around and become aware of how nature functions, we can see the metaphors everywhere, even with our beloved pets.

My dog was peacefully going through the death process during the winter holidays. I watched her sleeping as she lay comfortably on her bed, her chest slowly rising and falling with each shallow breath. Although the snowy winds were howling outside, we were warm in our house. I gently scratched her cheeks and the top of her head, which gave her so much pleasure. When she looked up at me, I could see the twinkling holiday lights reflecting in her eyes from the brightly decorated Yule tree just a few feet away.

Having been rescued from the animal shelter, she lived fifteen happy years with me in the country, running through the woods and wading in the shallow creek that flowed through the property. The memories of our adventures together started popping up like a slideshow. What stood out the most for me were the lessons I learned from her about living a more enjoyable life.

One of the lessons I learned was how to enjoy each day. She never took life for granted. She woke up in the morning with excitement for whatever the day may bring. The enthusiasm she showed as she ran out into the yard was unmatched. She treated every single day as a gift regardless of the weather. I would love to reach such a state of mind where I could go through my day with as much zeal and positive energy as my dog.

Additionally, I learned from her that it is not enough to enjoy only the big thrills in life; I also need to appreciate the smaller joys. Some of those little pleasures that she and I enjoyed together included sunshine, a pleasant breeze, praise, good food, a cool drink of water, a warm bed, eggrolls (oh, how she loved eggrolls), going for a ride in the car, a walk on the beach, and being spoken to in a friendly tone of voice. And, of course, the pleasure she liked the best of all was backrubs—lots and lots of backrubs!

Aren't these the things we all want? Do we appreciate all the wonderful things in our lives? If we don't, why not? Why do we postpone happiness? Do dogs delay joy? No way! That's why Mother Nature gave them tails to wag.

Life is not always blissful; my dog didn't like some things. Such as an angry tone of voice, hot and muggy summer days, too much commotion, and, worst of all, being ignored. My dog learned to adjust to the unpleasant aspects of life by either leaving the area or ignoring those objections.

Similarly, for us humans, there may be times when we get ignored at home or have too much commotion distracting us at work. There may be other times when people are talking in a hostile voice. At moments like this, we can remember our beloved pets and, like them, tune the objection out or, if possible, go into another room. Furthermore, many dogs possess desirable characteristics, which I am still trying to incorporate into my personality.

Here are some of my favorites:

- Dogs have loyalty. They do not abandon someone when times get tough. Maybe that's why divorcing couples fight for custody of the family dog. The dog was probably more loyal than the spouse.
- Dogs are quick to forgive. They do not judge or harbor resentment, hatred, or prejudice. I think the whole world needs to learn that lesson.

- Dogs live in the moment. They find joy in the here and now.
- Dogs let go of the past. As soon as the barking ends, they are so over it.

My dog taught me that every living being has an intrinsic value that cannot be bought, earned, bestowed, stolen, or taken away. It's just an innate part of being alive. My dog had value just for being and did not need to win the right to have worth. And so it is with you, too.

Today's Teaching from Mother Nature

Engage every situation with the enthusiasm of a dog. Get excited about the mundane, ordinary, simple things you might take for granted. Make a list of the things you find uninteresting in your daily routine. Then, behind each item, write down something you appreciate about that ordinary thing, perhaps something you hadn't noticed before. Take a fresh look at your life. In other words, live like a dog!

Remember, dogs also have the endearing quality of being so happy to see you when you come home that they jump for joy. You may have a horrible day, but that dog will still be thrilled to see you. And what is the result? You instantly feel better. There's nothing quite like unconditional love to improve your mood.

Now, show that same enthusiasm to the people in your life. How much happiness would it bring them if you smiled with joy upon seeing them? What about showing appreciation to everyone you come across in your day? It's a form of gratitude, and the world needs more. Since you can only control your behavior and not others, please don't wait for them to make the first move. You take the initiative and radiate unconditional love to those around you. What a wonderful world it could be!

51

As Genuine as a Colorful Sunrise

Over the years, I met several individuals who were so caught up in pretending to be someone else that they were not living genuine lives. They had abandoned their true nature. It was as though they were not fully alive. To the unsuspecting viewer, they looked alive but were not living authentically.

Consider the fictional story of a senior citizen named Jim. This man had a suicide attempt in which he'd intentionally driven off the road with his foot on the accelerator. He justified this reckless act because he was angry and didn't have what he thought he deserved from life. He believed that fate was out to get him. When he compared his life to the lives of those around him, he felt shortchanged. He thought he was entitled to have the luxurious life he saw on TV.

He survived the attempt and was not seriously injured. For months afterward, he obsessed about how he'd almost died. He couldn't get that thought out of his head. It appeared he hadn't considered his mortality and that his life would eventually end.

Let's pause now and review this case. From a certain point of view, the day he attempted suicide, his way of life came to an end, and he hasn't been authentically alive since. He was trying to live in the memories of the past and will continue to do so until he starts living an authentic life true to his nature. He needs to design a new life for himself rather than just live a life by default. It's as if his old life was a role in a play directed by society. Now, Jim needs to ask himself if this is a role he wants to keep playing.

Here's a second made-up example: As a child, Lora learned to be ashamed of her sexuality. In her childhood, she was taught that sex was a sin, and not just sexual acts, but sexual thoughts, too. According to Lora, even *feeling* a sexual desire was a sin. Consequently, she feared religious judgment and rejection. She would do anything to fit in with her cultish religious group, including denying her true nature and authentic feelings.

By her late teens, Lora was just a shell of a person, a chameleon pretending to be whatever her overcontrolling religious group told her to be. They even pressured her to abandon her dream of having a career. They wanted her to marry one of the older men in their group, who was three times her age, and raise a large family. She did not dare say that she was not even sexually attracted to men.

Lora always made a big deal out of celebrating her birthday. Ironically, she never noticed the incongruency between honoring her birth and, at the same time, dishonoring the person she was born to be. In other words, she was not living her life genuinely. She stopped being true to herself early in life and decided to become what others wanted her to be.

No doubt her group socially rewarded her with kudos for living up to their expectations, but there's just one problem with that: There is someone else Lora needed to be—her true self. That's the authentic role she was born to play. Let's give her the benefit of the doubt and assume she eventually gathers enough character strength to break away from her oppressors' control and embrace her true nature as a freethinking woman.

What about you? Are you living a life that is true to your nature? Many of us are like actors playing a role others designed for us. When we get together with our relatives, we sometimes put on fake smiles and say things we don't mean, like, "We should do this more often." Or, "Let's keep in touch." When someone tells an off-color joke at work that isn't funny, we laugh just because everyone else in the room is chuckling, no doubt giving the same phony laugh. We've played these roles for so long that we have forgotten our true selves.

Sometimes, we look at old pictures of ourselves and reminisce about our past. We miss the person we used to be. We were innocent, genuine, sincere, and uninhibited as children. We felt free to express our feelings. Back then, we were true to our nature. As adults, we pretend to be interested in things we are not and to like people we don't. Why have we become so disingenuous? We should take pride in how nature made us, just as the hummingbirds proudly display their colors, bright or dull.

What made us think that our true colors were somehow unacceptable? What was so terrible about who we were that made us suppress those personality traits deep within us? When does our true nature ever come out? Perhaps, in our dreams? Yes, that is when we can finally be our true selves. Our dreams are where our inner child can come out and play.

In dreams, we are natural. Nature is genuine. We can look to nature for examples of how to be authentic. A sunrise expresses its true colors. It does not mask anything nor pretend to be something else. The colors you see on the horizon are real, not fake. The sunrise is like a graphic display of colorful emotions: playful yellow, solemn orange, angry red, peaceful lavender, with a true-blue sky as a backdrop.

It is not too late for us. We can learn to connect with our true nature and reconnect with our childhood sincerity by being honest about how we feel. In other words, just as nature is genuine, we can learn to be more authentic in what we say, do, and live.

Living an authentic life does not mean we always need to say whatever thought comes into our minds, as an untrained child does. We still need to use self-discipline, discretion, and discernment. However, we can acknowledge our thoughts and feelings in the privacy of our minds instead of pretending that they don't exist. Then, upon reflection, we can decide what to do about those thoughts and feelings. That's where discretion comes in.

Today's Teaching from Mother Nature

Think about the otters for a minute. Otters are genuine. They do not pretend to be any other animal. They are true to themselves. When they play, they are like children or water acrobats as they roll, spin, and tumble in the waves. Let your authentic nature be as playful and free as the otters.

One way to stay in touch with your authentic inner child is to keep a dream journal or daydream diary. Write down what your nocturnal thoughts are communicating to you in your dreams. Particularly, pay attention to the softly spoken voice of your inner child. Let the essence of your colorful personality shine like a beautiful sunrise. That tiny voice in your mind reminds you of your authentic nature.

Your playful inner child is not asking you to act childishly; instead, it wants you to have the excitement of a curious child. Start paying attention to that calling. Gradually adjust your thoughts, behaviors, and personality as you progress toward a greater expression of your true self.

52
As Peaceful as a Watchful Owl

People occasionally ask me how they can remain peaceful when everyone around them is arguing. Sometimes, it can seem as though the whole world is fighting. There is ample chaos, whether at work, at home, or in society itself. Nonetheless, you can still learn ways to let your mind be as peaceful as the cottony plume of a dandelion seed with its parachute-like structure that floats effortlessly in the breeze.

Let's delve into this issue with an imaginary example about Chris. When Chris was a ten-year-old boy, he had a bad temper. He couldn't stop arguing with his family. Every order from his parents resulted in a defensive outburst. Any direction given to him was met with resistance.

Then, one evening, just after dusk, Chris spotted a barred owl in the woods. What he saw the owl doing changed his perspective forever, eventually curbing his angry outbursts. What was the owl doing that made such a powerful impression? Well, she wasn't doing anything. She was doing something by not doing something. In other words, the owl was silent and still yet mindfully observing things around her. She was a watcher. That descriptive title caught Chris's attention because it sounded like the name of a superhero, the Watcher. At that moment, his eyes grew as big as the owl's.

So, he pondered how to be more watchful of the things happening around him at home, especially just before a family fight started. Most of his childhood frustration stemmed from his impatience with family members doing things he didn't like. Specifically, Chris couldn't seem to handle the frustration of waiting. So, he realized that he, like the owl, could be a watcher and observe what was happening rather than getting angry.

After several months of practicing owl watchfulness, Chris was a little better at seeing the broader picture of what was going on in his home. He observed that his parents were busy with other responsibilities, and his siblings were caught up in their activities. By playing the role of the Watcher, he was starting to see that each family member had stuff going on. This was not to say he didn't still want his needs met; he was just more mindful now.

As Chris grew up, he continued to have occasional anger outbursts; however, they became less frequent. He was more watchful of the surrounding situation, which drew his attention away from his anger. In essence, he was developing an owllike view. Put another way, he was intensely watching something of interest while being aware of what was in his peripheral vision. To be clear, Chris still wanted to get his way, but now he was more aware of other activities on the fringe.

The next big hurdle was learning to be patient like the owl. This stage was challenging because, after all, Chris was full of youthful energy! He studied several pictures of owls in their natural habitat, usually sitting on branches. He saw how patient they were. As with the last lesson, it took him many months of trial and error before the new behavior became second nature. He had to keep reminding himself to be patient and count to ten instead of impulsively arguing with people.

Day by day, he slowly learned to manage his anger and develop owllike watchfulness and patience. There were, of course, plenty of times when Chris fell short of his ideals. However, those were the times for personal reflection to learn more about how the owl practices self-control by not trying to run everything around her. Since the wise bird does not need to control others, she focuses on being calm.

This inner balance allows the creature to silently be mindful of what is happening in the present moment.

Let's wrap this story up by saying that Chris is currently an adult and still practices these skills of silent observation and patience. At his place of employment, Chris consciously chooses to be reserved at first whenever an argument breaks out. Like the owl, he stops making a commotion and sits silently for several seconds, counting to ten in his head before talking. When he does speak, he only uses a few words, and that's it. Like the wind, he knows when to end. Even the breeze takes a break.

We can all practice this owl wisdom for the rest of our lives. And as time passes, we will learn life lessons along the way. Furthermore, we can study other animals and learn how to identify their favorable characteristics that can relate to people. Then, if we wish, we can write a journal about the new lessons we learned and reflect on them in daily meditation. Most importantly, we can continue to discover new ways to remain peaceful even amid chaos and conflicts.

Today's Teaching from Mother Nature

Unless it's an emergency, try to remain emotionally aloof during an argument as if you were an owl sitting on a branch being the curious watcher. Once you observe for a reasonable time, gather your thoughts and speak calmly or hoot softly.

You, too, can be an owllike observer (a watcher) with your family and coworkers. As you share your thoughts and feelings, don't demand they pay full attention to you; they may have other things going on in their peripheral vision. If they are not interested in your point of view, that's their right. No law states that they must be fascinated by everything you say. If they do not want to listen to you, be like the owl and fly silently to a more hospitable environment, perhaps among friends.

Acknowledge that you can only control yourself, not others. Just focus on managing your life. Feel as free as the owl to set your schedule and agenda. For instance, you can invite your family or coworkers to join you in your activities. If they accept, that's great. If not, that's okay, too, because you have the wisdom of the owl to understand that you can't change people against their will. Unfortunately, some may have to learn painful yet valuable life lessons from their mistakes. In the meantime, you can remain as peaceful as the owl despite the chaos.

Conculsion

I am proud of you for journeying through these chapters with me. Together, we explored a deeper level of our connection with nature. The stories I shared with you in this book covered more than ten years of emotionally connecting with the natural environment. I do not take credit for the wisdom of Mother Nature, only for *my* experience of Her. I was happy to share these woodland lessons with you, and I encourage you to discover your own when you continue to interact with nature in whatever way feels best for you.

You don't have to climb a mountain and talk to a sage sitting in the lotus position at the mouth of a cave to learn the teachings of Mother Earth. If you are able-bodied, stroll in the forest, park, or along the beach. If you are unable to go outside, enjoy the view from your window. Perhaps nature has a message for you when you observe the birds sitting patiently on the branches, the moon showing courage by coming out from behind the clouds, or the sun's warm rays gently providing nurturance and brightening everyone's day. Please, share your lessons.

Subject Chapter Index

Behaviors

Addiction

Assertiveness

Bad habits

Breathing

Perseverance

Self-nurturing

Emotions

Anger

Anxiety

Depression

Fear

Happiness

Self-acceptance

Stress

Metaphors

Birds (larger)

Birds (smaller)

Carnivores

Dog wisdom

Elements

Herbivores

Insects

Relationships

Family

Interconnectedness

Romantic

Thoughts

Forgiveness

Mindfulness

Perspective

Visualization Techniques

Guided imagery

Gratitude

I accomplish nothing in isolation. With that in mind, I express my heartfelt gratitude to my parents, ancestors, and mentors, including nonhuman teachers, such as animals, plants, elements, and the seasons. An enormous gratitude is extended to Grandmother Moon for guiding me and lighting my path at night and Grandfather Sun for warming me and lighting my path during the day.

Special thanks to the staff at Llewellyn Worldwide for their expertise and professionalism in preparing this book for publication. Specifically, I want to recognize Liz Stewart, acquisitions editor; Nanette Stearns, editorial director; Sami Sherratt, production editor; Shira Atakpu, art director; and Rordan Brasington, production designer. All your combined talents and creative energy made this project happen. Thank you for seeing the vision of this book.

I thank those who encouraged me over the years as I wrote this book. A particular note of appreciation goes to Michelle Rusk, Leslie Gramstrup, Jessica Biolo, Michelle Rochon, Matt Dietsche, Jenn Ellis, and all the supportive staff and faculty at Northwood Technical College. Empathic friends: Dennis Crumb, Gary Houdek, Flora Woodfork, and Mark Kirschieper. Compassionate allies: Beverly Berntson and the entire Iron Lotus meditation group. Spiritual companions: Helga Hedgewalker, Jerome Aubrey, Paula Morhardt, Paul B. Rucker, and the Pagan community. Merry we meet, merry we part, and merry we meet again.

To Write to the Author

If you wish to contact the author or would like more information about this book, please write to the author in care of Llewellyn Worldwide Ltd. and we will forward your request. Both the author and the publisher appreciate hearing from you and learning of your enjoyment of this book and how it has helped you. Llewellyn Worldwide Ltd. cannot guarantee that every letter written to the author can be answered, but all will be forwarded. Please write to:

Mark Langenfeld
℅ Llewellyn Worldwide
2143 Wooddale Drive
Woodbury, MN 55125-2989

Please enclose a self-addressed stamped envelope for reply, or $1.00 to cover costs. If outside the U.S.A., enclose an international postal reply coupon.

Many of Llewellyn's authors have websites with additional information and resources. For more information, please visit our website at https://www.llewellyn.com.